THE
TOTAL TOWN MAKEOVER

Other books by Andrew McCrea

The American Countryside,

The Man Who Was President for a Day,

God's Perfect View, and

Making Molehills out of Mountains

THE
TOTAL TOWN
MAKEOVER

RETHINKING BUSINESS, COMMUNITY, AND HOME IN SMALL-TOWN AMERICA

ANDREW McCREA

BLAKE
&KING

Maysville, Missouri

Published by Blake & King
4663 State Hwy A
Maysville, MO 64469

Publisher's Cataloging-in-Publication Data
McCrea, Andrew, 1972–

The total town makeover : rethinking business, community, and home in small-town America / Andrew McCrea. – Maysville, MO : Blake & King, 2019.

p. ; cm.

ISBN13: 978-0-9725331-9-5

1. Rural development—United States. 2. Community development—United States. 3. Economic development—United States. 4. Small cities--United States. I. Title.

HN49.C6 M33 2019
307.14—dc23   2019930100

First Edition

Project coordination by Jenkins Group, Inc.
www.bookpublishing.com

Design by Yvonne Fetig Roehler

Printed in the United States of America
23 22 21 20 19 • 5 4 3 2 1

Dedication

To Paula, Luke, and Alison.
I love you.

Masontown
Fairchance
Fort Necessity NB
Meyersdale
Petersburg
West Virginia
Luray
Harrisonburg
Bridgewater
Verona
Staunton
Waynesboro
Summersville
Lewisburg
Clifton Forge
Ronceverte
Covington
Buena Vista
Virg
Lynchburg
Princeton
Hollins
Timberlake
Bluefield
Blacksburg
Salem
Roanoke
Radford
Pulaski
Christiansburg
Altavista
Wytheville
Hillsville
Collinsville
Martinsville
Galax
Danville
Toast
Mount Airy
Eden
Mayodan
Roxboro
King
Reidsville
Elkin
Stanleyville

Contents

Minnesota
Iowa
Fairmont
Albert Lea
Austin
Wells
Estherville
Lake Mills
Northwood
Osage
Forest City
Mason City
Algona
Britt
Garner
Charles City
Belmond
Humboldt
Clarion
Hampton
Fort Dodge
Cedar F
Rockwell City
Webster City
Eldora
Story City
Carroll
Ames
Nevada
Marshallto
Jefferson
Tama
Madrid
Perry
Ankeny
Grinnell
dubon
Urbandale
Colfax
Newton
Des Moines
Norwalk
Pella
Indianola
Greenfield
Winterset
Knoxville
Creston
Osceola
Chariton
Albia

Preface

The events in this book are real-life stories, most of which are based on personal interviews I've conducted, on location, with those creating positive change in the places they live. I've chosen not to place footnotes in the book because so many of the examples are based on these personal conversations.

In most cases, I've identified the people being interviewed and where they live. However, in a few cases, I've omitted the name, place, or identifying details because sensitive or critical information was shared. The purpose is to provide true stories that will be helpful to others but not to share details that could hurt those willing to share challenging situations they've overcome.

This book also draws on others' research and writings on the subject. See the bibliography in the back of the book, which lists these resources that might be helpful in the quest to create a total town makeover.

Prologue

What is a large city? As a kid, I thought a "large" city was any place with a fast-food restaurant or a Walmart. Those cities had everything you could ever want or need in life.

The closest town to our farm in northwest Missouri didn't have either of these big-city "luxuries." Neither did our entire county, for that matter. In fact, my *county* didn't have a stoplight, unless you counted the one that blinked yellow at the main intersection in town.

Conversely, a small town was the place where I went to school—and whom we competed against in sports. Those towns had a one- or two-block main street. The schools graduated fewer than 50 students from high school each year.

The difference between "large" and "small" towns is primarily defined by where we grew up. I struggled with the subtitle of this book because defining "small-town America" is a matter of opinion. I settled on the answer that small-town America can be found anywhere in the nation. By all accounts, the place where I grew up is a small town. In fact, my entire *county* has just 6,500 residents.

"Small town" can also be used to describe smaller areas or neighborhoods within larger cities. For instance, Westchester County, New York, which is just north of the Bronx, the northernmost borough of New York City, has just under one million residents. Within that county, though, you will find Tarrytown and Sleepy Hollow, each with a population of about 15,000. Tarrytown still has a volunteer fire department and many qualities of a small town.

In my mind, a small town is a place where local citizens live, work, go to school, play, and pray together. It is a place small enough most people know one another yet large enough to get things done. Regardless of the size of your town, this book should provide insights you can use.

Rural America is my home. Most of my travels have taken me to small towns. They are the places were the local barber is one of the most important people in town, not because he cuts your hair but because he has a 15-minute conversation with almost everyone in town every four weeks and can tell you most of the news you need—or don't need—to know. Small towns are places where you can't put too many people in the annual homecoming parade or there won't be enough people to actually stand on the side of the street and watch it go by.

Small towns are the greatest places on earth to raise a family because everyone knows one another. Small towns are the worst places on earth to raise a family because everyone knows one another. This book is really about two ways to view the place you live. Either way you look at it, you're correct. It's your job—and mine—to make our towns be the best places they can be.

I remember sitting in the local café in our small town with my family late one afternoon sometime in the mid-1980s. Directly across the street a crane was removing the clock from the side of the old two-story bank building. The bank had closed, a victim of the decade's farm crisis. The lady in the booth next to us looked at me and said, "Young man, never forget this day. That's a piece of history that's never coming back."

Around that same time, my family made our monthly trip to St. Joseph, Missouri, which was the "big city" to me. Mom would shop at the mall while my dad, sister, and I went to the bookstore. After that, we ate at Burger King before making the 50-minute drive back home.

One Saturday was different, though. We walked into Burger King, but Dad never stepped up to the cashier. He stared at the menu board for the longest time. He finally turned to Mom, whispered something to her, and walked out of the restaurant.

Mom bent down to my sister and me and said, "Kids, we're going to McDonald's. Burger King has raised their prices."

I will always remember that moment—and can still picture it as clear in my mind as the day it took place. I'm not exaggerating when I say I lived the next decade of my life without setting foot in a Burger King. That was where people with money ate.

We weren't poor. We weren't staring at foreclosure. But times were tough. Dad never said a word about it. He remained positive. He never gave us a reason to fear.

Perhaps that's why I'm an optimist, which is a blessing and a curse. I like to imagine things for the better. But when those things don't go as planned, they often crush you even more. Being an optimist doesn't mean you ignore the negative; it simply means you choose to see issues with two sides in the best way possible. Why not look for the positive? This book chooses to take that view while recognizing the challenges that must be overcome.

There are several books that take a more negative view on rural and small-town America. There's truth in the trends, statistics, and real-life examples they share, which I'll discuss in this book. You can't ignore the truth, but you can choose to create a better one.

Through the years, I have served on various boards that seek to improve the health and well-being of our region and state. We must think beyond our city limits—county, state, and even global perspectives are important. Otherwise, we will lose sight of the bigger picture around us.

That said, I believe we often miss the importance of the "small" or "local" view. It's not "small" because it's narrow, uninformed, or rigid. It's "small" from the standpoint of looking at how local successes change towns for the better in a relatively short amount of time. This book is also about how the small/local view makes the bigger view even better.

I started working on this book a couple of decades ago without realizing it. For more than 20 years, I've hosted a syndicated radio and television feature that mostly focuses on ordinary people and places doing extraordinary things. The people I interview are often from small towns. Listeners and viewers have told me they find inspiration in these stories.

As the months and years passed, I really didn't think about the stories as a whole as inspirational—I was simply sharing one story after another. As I reflect now, perhaps we were accomplishing something larger. We were telling the real-life stories of people living in small-town America who were positively influencing the place they lived.

This book is about how people and towns are making themselves better. In some cases, one person can do it, and the difference can be remarkable in a short amount of time. Some small towns will survive and thrive. Some will not. The fate of those places is greatly influenced by how you choose to look at it and what you choose to do about it.

Several years ago, while serving on a local planning board, we were discussing a program we were going to create in our town. One person said, "We can't be as good as the program they have in that town." After all, *that* town was four times the size of our town.

I replied, "Why not? Why can't we be just as good?"

Can you imagine a high school basketball coach telling his or her team they couldn't win? Would a football coach tell his or her high school team they should only hope to win a couple of games in a season? Of course not! We cheer on our local high school sports teams with the hope they can beat even the best teams. So why put limits on the place you live?

Small towns believe they have a chance to beat just about anyone is sports. Why do those same towns believe they can't win when it comes to more important matters, such as creating the best schools, businesses, churches, and civic groups? This book features people and places that are hard to find on a map. The people didn't look at their town and see the reasons they couldn't make it better—they saw all the reasons why they could make it better!

A few years ago, my dad and I were looking to buy another ranch horse. We still regularly ride horses to check and herd our cattle. A friend of ours, Jack, owns and trains horses at his livestock auction, and he had a horse he thought would be a good buy for us. Jack is a great guy who loves life and always seems to be upbeat, even in the toughest of times.

He took us to a pen and showed us a small, thin Quarter Horse. "This horse really knows how to work around cattle," Jack said. "We've been roping big steers off him. We take him by himself in the pasture, and he does great all the time. He's a real go-getter!"

Dad looked at the horse with skepticism. He certainly didn't have the frame or muscles to hold his ground with a large steer on the other end of the rope. Dad laughed and said, "Jack, that horse is too little to do that work!"

Jack smiled and said, "That horse doesn't know he's little!"

You—and your town—are only little and limited if you think you are. You'll be amazed at what you can do. Here's a look at several people and places that chose to be a much bigger horse than they appear to be.

Chapter 1

Vision of the Future

It was the heart of the Depression. The Dust Bowl was wreaking havoc in middle America. At the time, my now neighbor was a young farmer simply hoping to survive.

"I can't describe just how bad it was," says Billy, now sharing the story about six decades after it took place. "It was like a fog, a bad fog." The dust would roll in like a wave in an ocean. However, this wave was blistering heat and wind, filled with the grit of soil and sand carried from some faraway place, sweeping through fields of withering crops.

"Forty acres was a good-size field for one man," says Billy. "I told myself, 'If one man can plant 40 acres, well, I can do 80!'" He was resilient, too young to know better, and intent on battling the elements of Mother Nature to build the farm to support his family.

"I did plant 80 acres and did a right good job of it too—and that fall I could have carried every ear of corn I raised in one burlap bag, if I could have found it all."

It was against that backdrop that Billy's brother, Maurice, two years his elder, was attempting to build his own farm. Maurice worked with his father-in-law, Mr. Loest, on local projects off the farm as well.

Billy, Maurice, and Mr. Loest were a bit different from many others in their community—in a good way. They were young and progressively minded and perhaps naive enough to believe they could outwork and outthink the challenges stacked against them.

In fact, Maurice bought the very first tractor with rubber tires in the area—although the tractor was ordered incorrectly and showed up with rubber instead of steel tires. Everyone thought it would be a bust and the rubber tires would just spin in the soil compared with the steel that would grab the earth and spin a tractor at the end of the field rows.

Despite what the neighbors thought, the rubber tires worked. Maurice was a farmer full of ideas. In fact, the local newspaper had an account of how he was doing field work in the middle of the night by the light of the moon. It was his way to avoid the heat, keep his draft stock cool, and accomplish more.

Based on the success of what had the potential to be their biggest blunder, Maurice and Mr. Loest decided to go door-to-door selling a product in the middle of the worst economic and agricultural downturn anyone alive had ever seen.

Both men worked up a sales pitch detailing why people should spend what little money they had on something that could revolutionize their homes, farms, and communities.

The routine was simple: Get up early and take care of the farm chores. Pack a sack lunch and drive to a nearby town. Once there, they would divide the town into two halves and knock on the doors of every household.

Some days their efforts went well. Other days were disheartening. The door-to-door work reached a boiling point one hot afternoon in a little town on Missouri's Grand River. The pair rolled into the town with the goal of selling the product to everyone. After knocking on the doors, they met back at the city park to eat their lunch before heading home.

Feigning interest and hope, Maurice said to Mr. Loest, "How'd you do today? Sell a lot of people?

"Not a single one, Maurice," he said. "Not a single one."

As the older generation, Mr. Loest perhaps felt guilty. He should have known better than to lead his son-in-law on a fool's errand such as this. No one needed to spend time away from the farm, especially if it was to be wasted touting the merits of something people weren't inspired to buy.

At that point, something ignited within Maurice. It was an impulse he'd tried to tamp down, but now it had burst into flame. Like his father-in-law, Maurice was disappointed. The pain from lost time away from his farm and his family stung. There was nothing to do but simply let go of the disappointment that consumed him after going door to door and being rejected every single time.

"What are we doing here?" Maurice thundered. "Why are we doing this? People don't care. People don't believe. People can't see any reason why they need what we have!"

Maurice could have stopped, but the passion within him was ablaze—there was no squelching it. "We aren't going to save our farms; we're going to lose them. This is a waste of time . . . of money . . . of life!"

The tirade was directed at the town, but it was delivered in the presence of just one man, Mr. Loest. Those who had rejected Maurice had long since gone back inside their house or to the barn, not to waste more time on silly ideas that cost precious money.

The one man who believed in the product as Maurice did was the only soul to hear the sermon preached in the park that day. It didn't really matter, though. Anyone who was within earshot would have just chalked it up as two angry men who were lousy salesmen.

There was silence as Maurice ran out of words to describe his anger and frustration. Mr. Loest paused too, wondering whether there would be more to his son-in-law's rant or whether this was the end.

The silence lasted for a long time. Mr. Loest felt compelled to say something, but he didn't know what to say. His son-in-law was justified in being upset, yet he needed to provide him with hope.

"Maurice," he said, looking at his son-in-law for the first time since sitting down on the park bench. " "Remember: sometimes it just takes a little time for people to believe."

It takes time for people to believe? How long might it take? Would they believe in his lifetime? Would they believe in time to make any difference?

As the two men picked up their sack lunches to head home, Maurice couldn't shake the reason each household gave for their lack of interest. Money wasn't the issue this time. People weren't buying because they didn't see the value of the product and what it could do for them.

So . . . what was the product Maurice and Mr. Loest were going door-to-door selling? Electricity. They were selling shares in the Rural Electric Association so homes could get electricity. But on that day, every single person looked Maurice square in the eye and said, "Electricity? I doubt I'll ever use it."

Perhaps you've already guessed that Billy and Maurice were more than just characters in this real-life story. Maurice McCrea was my grandfather, and Billy was his brother. My grandfather was born in 1903, before the first airplane took flight. Sixty-six years later, he saw a man on the moon. He had witnessed a lot of change.

The rejection he encountered in the small river town because the people didn't want to buy electricity continued to bother him for years to come. It wasn't about the money—the vision was lacking. The people simply could not, or refused to, see how electricity could change their lives. There are ways to scrape together money, but if there's no vision, a person and a place begin to perish from within.

Identifying the Need

So, what's your vision for the town you call home? What positive strides can you take to benefit the place you live?

If you don't see a need to change, you probably won't. The same goes for communities, counties, and regions. If there's not a compelling reason to change, most people are content with the status quo. In this book, we'll primarily focus on small towns and cities in rural America. If you live in such a place, some of the following facts should provide compelling evidence to create change.

Perhaps we should first begin with the question posed in the prologue. "What is a small town, and what is a rural area?" It's difficult to draw an exact line on what divides large cities, small towns, and rural areas. According to the U.S. Census Bureau, 97% of the land area in the United States is considered rural, which is home to 19.3% of the population, or about 60 million residents.

Put another way, there are slightly more than 3,100 counties, parishes, and county equivalents in the United States, according to the Census Bureau. Of those counties, 704 are considered 100% rural. The largest is Lincoln County, Maine, with a population of nearly 35,000 people. On the flip side, Loving County, Texas, has but 82 residents. More than 20% of the population in the United States resides in the 704 rural counties.

Here's where the lines begin to blur. There are counties considered to be "mostly rural" and even "mostly urban" that contain small towns. As mentioned earlier, Westchester County, New York, has nearly a million residents, but if you stroll down a street in Tarrytown (population of about 15,000) you'll experience quintessential small-town charm.

Rural America and small towns represent a significant percentage of our population and our land area, which is why they need to be strong and vibrant. Large and small towns can learn from each other. The stories and information in this book are not exclusive to a specific land or population size.

Our focus is on "small-town America," so let's look at how it compares to larger population centers in the country. According to Census Bureau data, in 1980, the median age of those living in small towns and rural areas was just over 30 years old. That figure was nearly identical to the median age of those living in large metro areas. By 2015, the median age in small towns and rural areas had increased to 41 years or older, while the figure for large metro areas was under 35 years. And the gap continues to widen.

While metro areas and suburbs have always had a higher percentage of residents with college degrees, the gap is widening when compared with small towns and rural areas.

In 1980, rural residents were generally healthier than those in cities when considering cardiovascular disease and cancer mortality. By 2015, the tables had turned. Tobacco use is higher in many rural areas, and the rate of chronic lung disease is widening, with rural areas falling further behind their city cousins. In general, many small towns and rural areas aren't as healthy, have lower incomes, and have less formal education than those in the large metro areas and suburbs.

While the birth rate in metros, suburbs, and rural areas has declined in the past decade, something significant is about to occur in rural America. The rate of deaths is ready to eclipse the rate of births, which hasn't happened in rural America, as a whole, since the initial European settlement of the nation.

Based on these trends, it might be accurate to say small towns and rural America are literally dying. Think about that for a moment. The place that more than 20% of Americans call home is dying.

I don't like writing that statement, because small towns and rural America are my home. The facts are there, but the fate is in question. Some of those towns and counties are withering away to become a new generation of ghost towns. However, others are reversing the trend and drawing new people, businesses, and schools. Either way your town looks at it, they're probably correct.

Leading the charge to ensure your town thrives really begins by asking two important questions:

1. *What needs to happen?*
2. *Who will make it happen?*

All of us can probably look around our town and see lots of ways to make it better. However, it's usually one or two pressing questions that need to be answered. Sometimes the question is suddenly thrust upon a community. Maybe a business closes or a historic building is in danger of being razed. Something needs to be done immediately to help save jobs or a historic structure.

In most cases, though, individuals and communities have time to find answers. The challenge is that the problems those places are facing often must come to a critical head before something is done. It's difficult to muster support for a cause until there's a sense of immediacy. The goal is to create teams of people who anticipate those needs and begin to act while solutions and time are still adequate.

What needs to happen? Be specific. List one to four bullet points of the most pressing needs of your town.

See The Need—Fill The Need

As a whole, rural America is now older, sicker, and poorer, comparatively speaking, than it was a few decades ago. Young people are leaving to build homes and careers elsewhere. Most rural counties have seen a decline in population, and storefronts that were once occupied on main street are now half vacant or worse.

It's the continuation of a trend that for many rural towns began in the 1980s. Lowell Kruse came to St. Joseph, Missouri, a Midwest city of about 75,000 people, in 1984 to become the CEO of the newly formed Heartland Hospital.

"The farm crisis was effecting the area," says Kruse. It was part of the reason the two hospitals in town were merging. The demand for two such facilities in a town of that size was lacking.

The financial situation at the new hospital was problematic. When Kruse came on board at the hospital, the facility had less than one day's operating funds on hand. He noticed that delivery trucks would stay parked at the loading docks for long periods of time. He later learned they were getting their money before unloading their product. Times were tough, not only on the farm but also for many businesses and organizations in the heartland.

But Kruse soon noticed something else in the area. "I was struck by the rate of heart disease, cancer, and diabetes," he says. "Just by looking at the numbers, you could tell we had an aging population."

For Kruse it became a "burning platform," which should be true for others when they recognize a negative trend. "Communities that don't pick up the challenge on this [reversing the negative trends in rural areas] will find themselves in a world of hurt. Some communities will make it, just like some people make it and others will not," he adds.

But turning around a community might involve working with some groups that have been bitter rivals. For longtime residents of rural communities, the one great rallying point is the local school. The school—especially its sports teams—is revered. Those who win championships are remembered, forever.

For generations, kids are told the stories behind the teams that appear on banners hanging in the high school gym. Twenty years before I began kindergarten, my school's football team went undefeated, and their opponents went scoreless the entire season. That's quite an accomplishment and one that should be remembered.

However, those rivalries sometimes get in the way of regional progress. When you have more deaths than births and you have more people going than coming, those barriers can become even greater challenges to communities that can't see past the rivalries. There must be a comradery to raise the well-being of a region.

It's hard for some towns in rural America to change their mind-set based on what might seem to be, at least on the surface, friendly sports rivalries, says Kruse. "It may mean we have to think differently about our neighboring communities we compete against and now we've got to work with. We have to think regionally and act locally," he says.

For those communities that can put some of those barriers behind them and see the bigger picture, there are opportunities for positive change.

But there's another challenge afoot—some towns and counties have grown in population. The number of businesses has increased since the farm crisis of the 1980s. They are "thriving" in comparison to other towns. But that can create a false sense of security, which can prove fatal as well.

Consider this: 30 miles up the road from the hospital Kruse managed is Maryville, Missouri, with a population of about 12,000. It's also home to Northwest Missouri State University. More than 6,000 students call the campus home each fall and spring. You'll find a community that is in many regards forward-thinking, with good schools and opportunities for people of all ages.

I recently spoke with Maryville leaders, who did note the population was projected to rise by 3% by the year 2030. Three percent isn't a big number, but it's a positive number, which is quite an accomplishment in rural America, especially considering Maryville is about 100 miles from urban centers in Omaha or Kansas City. The fact the town is growing is great news.

Maryville, Missouri, is the county seat of Nodaway County and home to Northwest Missouri State University. The city's population is expected to grow by 3% in the next 10 years; however, the community will lose $100 million in payroll by 2030 due to population loss in adjacent counties. *Photo courtesy Bridget Holtman Kenny*

However, when city and county planners look at the larger area of Nodaway, Atchison, Holt, Gentry, and Worth Counties, which have long provided labor to the area and whose citizens purchase retail goods in Maryville, the population of those counties is projected to significantly shrink.

If the projections hold true, economic planners in Maryville expect that the population decline will result in a loss of approximately $100 million in payroll. As one economic developer told me: "This is the reason we have to think regionally. If we focus only on our assigned areas, then we miss the bigger picture. Maryville and Nodaway County [Maryville is the county seat of Nodaway County] are connected to the surrounding counties, and if they are suffering, we will suffer as well."

Think of those towns and counties as islands, slowing sinking into the water. The surrounding counties will experience more deaths than births. Great young minds will move away. The population centers in those regions, cities such as Maryville, will stay above water longer than surrounding communities, but they will slowly lose ground, or at the very least not thrive.

Make no mistake: there's a need, a "burning platform" as Kruse calls it, that must be addressed. Rural and small-town America are crossing a threshold from which some say there's no turning back. The good news is I have seen towns, counties, and regions make the turnaround. They're the ones that accomplished a Total Town Makeover.

What does it take to buck the trend and lift people and places to success? It begins with people willing to take action. Is that "who" you?

What do you believe in? What vision do you have for yourself or your community that you wish to make a reality?

My grandfather was a forward-thinking man, and he realized electricity could do so much for his farm and those around him. The fact that others couldn't see that same vision was extremely frustrating for him. He would have understood if people couldn't afford it because times where tough and money was scarce. He could not fathom a lack of vision to see the opportunities. How could people think of electricity as something they'd never use?

The first step is realizing you have an important question that needs answering. The next step is determining who will move forward and take the lead.

The situation can seem daunting and the task too large for any one person, Kruse says. "Particularly in rural America, it's really, really important for people to believe they can do something about the situation," he says. "I know people in rural America are like, 'Wow, where's this all going?' but I've basically said to people, 'Help is not on the way.' The best help we've got is found in our local communities."

Kruse is correct. Help is not on the way in the form of a governmental program; however, local communities can make the difference. There are several resources, many of which communities either undervalue or don't know exist. Margaret Mead once said, "Never doubt that a small group of thoughtful, committed citizens can change the world; indeed, it's the only thing that ever has." It is those small groups that help make things happen.

So how do you mobilize that small but mighty force? Ron Drake knows the trials and tribulations of revitalizing a town. He moved to Siloam Springs, Arkansas, more than two decades ago. Drake has a knack for seeing the potential in older properties and has built a successful business flipping houses.

We met at one of the properties he renovated, a large home built in 1913 in downtown Siloam that had been converted to office space. It was a great example of what can be done with older properties in the "downtown" of small towns.

A local citizen once asked Drake why he didn't try to flip some downtown buildings to help bring small businesses back. It sounded like a reasonable request, so he set out looking for suitable properties to restore.

He hit a snag when it came to financing. His banker said, "Ron, even if someone gave you these properties, I couldn't loan you the money to renovate them." So Drake began to find people who had a shared vision for the old storefronts and began to partner with them on projects.

"What I've found is there are people in every community who have the ability to do great things. It's just inspiring them, convincing them, or showing them the numbers work," says Drake. He now works almost exclusively with small towns and knows the challenges—and opportunities—each location faces.

"Ironically, the biggest challenge a small town has is a psychological one; it's mental one," he says. "Downtown restoration is not brick-and-mortar but the restoration of the mind and believing it's possible in your town."

According to Drake, small towns often have two mental blocks. The older generation saw what the town once was and believes it can never return to that state of vitality. "They remember watching their downtown die," he says. "That is very difficult to erase and believe that your downtown can come back to life."

The younger generation has grown up hearing the stories of what the town once was, but they believe such turnarounds happen only in larger cities far from where they live. The biggest challenge is a mental one.

Don't get me wrong. You can't dismiss the challenges and let negativity go unchecked. There are hurdles. In some cases, those hurdles are tall, but there are towns taking extraordinary measures to leap those challenges and create a better future.

What sets the extraordinary communities apart from the ordinary ones? Certainly, you will find people committed to changing the fortunes of their town, but I have found the work of these extraordinary places can be divided into three main areas:

1. Economic Vitality
2. Vibrant Communities
3. Next-Generation Focus

You'll find many towns experiencing a total town makeover are organizing positive initiatives in all three of these areas.

As I often share with audiences, you have two ways to view rural and small-town America: first, it's slowly dying, businesses and young people are leaving, and the town's legacy is crumbling and, second, these locations are vibrant and full of economic opportunities where young families can live in an idyllic lifestyle. Either view you choose can be correct.

There are communities that fit both of the above descriptions. So what separates one from the other? Many books and research studies provide the statistics behind what's happening. I will occasionally refer to those trends as they establish an important statistical foundation for the topic at hand.

However, from my experiences, people want hope far more than numbers and trend lines. Hope. They want stories and examples that show a better future is attainable and here's how. They want to see other people and places are overcoming the odds to accomplish something great. Let's dive into those three areas and learn how some real-world examples are creating a better place to live and work. These are the people and places that confound the statistics and show us what we can become—something extraordinary.

CHAPTER 2

Strong Economies

I s there a perfect example of a "total town makeover"? My quest to find such a town began in a place outsiders might say was dying: Shickley, Nebraska.

"We're a town of 340 people," said Richard Walter, as we sat down to visit in the local library on main street. In Shickley, which is about 90 minutes southwest of Lincoln, there's only one "main street," which contains all the businesses within a three-block stretch. "We're a town that's close-knit and has a lot of pride," Richard said.

That wasn't always the case, though. In the late 1990s, a conversation at the local coffee shop, shortly after a prominent citizen passed away, proved vital to the future of the town. "One of our area bankers said, 'I always get tired of people coming into town for a funeral at 10 in the morning, at 1 they're at the bank cashing in all the CDs, and then we see their taillights heading out of the town, and that's the last we see of them,'" Richard recalled.

While the relatives had every right to do with their inheritance as they wished, it bothered some residents they never shared the story of Shickley with those generations that now lived many miles or states away. In fact, to secure the future, they needed to start celebrating the past and promoting the merits of the town with those who called Shickley home.

But how does a small town start such a campaign? How do you convince people their wealth should be invested in a place that some might say is on its way out? A few residents of Shickley hosted a town hall meeting in 2001 to help get things rolling—and the community saw a compelling need to do something to bolster their town.

They decided to establish an endowment through the Shickley Community Foundation. Richard is one of the board members. The board would raise money for the endowment. The interest from the funds would be used to support local projects, but the principle would never be touched.

In 2001, the Shickley Community Foundation became an affiliate of the Nebraska Community Foundation, which provided guidance and expertise to grow Shickley's reach and tell their story. At the same time, the Wilkens family, who owned the local bank, proposed a challenge. For every dollar the community raised, the bank would match it dollar for dollar, up to $105,000.

The town of Shickley not only matched it but also surpassed the mark, for a total of about $270,000. That money was the beginning of Shickley's endowment.

"The matching grants have been a very powerful tool for us because we're a very competitive community," Richard said. Shickley went on to apply for and receive matching grants from other organizations and foundations outside of the area.

The board made it their goal to visit with every family who lived in the school district. They also reached out to alumni who had moved away and others with ties to the small farming community. They were often amazed by where the donations would come from. Sometimes checks arrived from folks they didn't know who lived states away—people who had heard of the town's efforts and wanted to support the place that touched their lives.

During my visit with Richard, he made an important point many communities often forget: "The perception is out there that rural communities are drying up and dying. That's not the case. There's a lot of wealth in these rural communities. It's not in cash. It's in ag ground and assets like that."

Agricultural land values have increased several-fold since the dark days of the 1980s farm crisis. That wealth, even though it doesn't often change hands, and the landowners are the lifeblood of rural towns.

However, they won't give to a local cause if there's no one to tell the story and shepherd the projects or funds.

Recognizing the tremendous opportunity, Richard said, the Shickley Community Foundation set out to benefit from the transfer of wealth to come.

For a better understanding of the wealth in rural America and its transfer from one generation to the next, some organizations conduct Transfer of Wealth (TOW) studies. One such group is the Community Foundation of Northwest Missouri (CFNWMO).

Gentry County, Missouri, is a little over an hour's drive straight north of Kansas City. It has no stoplights. It's an agricultural county of just over 6,000 residents. The number of cattle and hogs in the county easily outnumbers the residents. Those not working the land or caring for livestock likely commute to larger towns in neighboring counties for work.

On the surface, Gentry County looks like much of rural America. It's a place with a rich farming history, yet the population is declining. Its residents' average income and education level fall below the state average.

However, Gentry County, like many other rural counties, has a lot of wealth. Say that to residents of the county and they might laugh, but the fact is one Richard discovered in Shickley. Opportunities abound for those who tell their story and get about the business of a total county makeover.

According to a TOW study conducted in 2016 (see figure on following page), land and businesses in Gentry County are valued at $450 million. During the next 10 years, by 2026, $160 million of that value is expected to transfer from one generation to the next.

TRANSFER OF WEALTH (TOW)

Area	Current Value (Billions)	10-Year TOW			50-Year TOW		
		10-Year Value (Billions)	5% Capture Value (Millions)	5% Payout (Millions)	50-Year Value (Billions)	5% Capture Value (Millions)	5% Payout (Millions)
Missouri	$517.70	$134.97	$6,748.58	$337.43	$1,510.53	$75,526.30	$3,776.31
Northwest MO	$18.06	$5.38	$268.72	$13.43	$51.37	$2,567.69	$128.38
Andrew	$1.66	$0.40	$20.09	$1.00	$4.13	$206.55	$10.33
Atchison	$0.41	$0.14	$6.79	$0.34	$1.02	$51.02	$2.55
Buchanan	$6.04	$1.77	$88.61	$4.43	$18.57	$928.52	$46.43
Caldwell	$0.62	$0.18	$8.78	$0.44	$1.71	$85.26	$4.26
Clinton	$1.85	$0.43	$21.52	$1.08	$4.44	$221.89	$11.09
Daviess	$0.61	$0.19	$9.57	$0.48	$1.59	$79.34	$3.97
Dekalb	$0.60	$0.17	$8.29	$0.41	$1.66	$82.80	$4.14
Gentry	$0.45	$0.16	$7.94	$0.40	$1.13	$56.51	$2.83
Grundy	$0.58	$0.21	$10.41	$0.52	$1.69	$84.34	$4.22
Harrison	$0.56	$0.20	$9.91	$0.50	$1.60	$79.85	$3.99
Holt	$0.34	$0.12	$6.21	$0.31	$1.16	$57.99	$2.90
Linn	$0.83	$0.26	$13.08	$0.65	$1.99	$99.45	$4.97
Livingston	$1.03	$0.37	$18.27	$0.91	$3.27	$163.50	$8.17
Mercer	$0.27	$0.09	$4.26	$0.21	$0.73	$36.42	$1.82
Nodaway	$1.35	$0.44	$21.99	$1.10	$4.91	$245.39	$12.27
Putnam	$0.37	$0.11	$5.68	$0.28	$0.85	$42.63	$2.13
Sullivan	$0.32	$0.09	$4.59	$0.23	$0.54	$27.09	$1.35
Worth	$0.17	$0.05	$2.73	$0.14	$0.38	$19.14	$0.96

In 2013, the Community Foundation of Northwest Missouri Inc., in partnership with the Alliance of Missouri Community Foundations and Missouri USDA Rural Development, conducted a Transfer of Wealth (TOW) study. The data show how much wealth will transfer in each county of Missouri in the next 10 years and 50 years (10-year value and 50-year value). The data above, for counties in northwest Missouri, also show the economic impact if 5% of the TOW was "captured" (5% capture value) and placed into an endowment fund, resulting in an annual payout locally (5% payout).

Part of CFNWMO's mission is to share the impact of thinking locally when transferring that wealth. For example, in their presentations CFNWMO staff often ask landowners: When passing land on to your children, would you consider setting aside a small portion to be invested in your community? Would you be willing to give 5%?

As you can see in the table, 5% of $160 million is $8 million. If that $8 million was invested in an endowment, as the town of Shickley did, Gentry County, Missouri, could expect to receive $400,000 per year, every year, in perpetuity.

Let's not skip over this fact too quickly or dismiss it as unattainable. If residents gave 5% of the transfer of wealth to local causes and that money was invested in an endowment, organizations would have $400,000 per year to support local causes. That money is in addition to any the county is already raising via taxes and other donations to charitable causes.

Take the TOW study one step further. In the next 50 years, Gentry County will have approximately $1.13 billion change hands. Capturing 5% of that total would result in a fund of more than $56 million, which would pay out nearly $3 million each year, forever.

As Richard said, "There's a lot of wealth in these rural communities." Remember: Gentry County doesn't have any large cities, and its calculated wealth is easily under that of most counties. The potential is there. You don't have to capture even 5%. Just go catch "some" percent.

I was recently visiting with a bank president who oversaw several branches in an agricultural area. He started working for the bank in the early 1980s. Although he had moved up the ranks, the original branch he oversaw was still in his area, and he kept tabs on its performance.

"You know that branch bank only has about half the amount of deposits it had when I was there," he remarked. He was not inferring the local leadership was ineffective or they were losing deposits to rivals. He was simply stating the income derived from farming in the area was being deposited somewhere else, often many miles away in larger communities.

Keep in mind: farmland in the area had increased many times during the 30-year period; however, the money deposited in the bank had dropped by half. The money was leaving town. The wealth was leaving the area. As Shickley, Nebraska, realized, a town must share its story and provide a reason for the wealth to be invested back into the community, especially in times when the population is holding constant, at best, or, in most cases, declining.

Shickley, Nebraska, formed a local community foundation to raise endowment funds to help with future projects. Local citizens have shared their vision for the community's future and as a result now have an endowment projected to reach $8 million.

The story of Shickley stuck with me after my initial interview several years ago. I was inspired to give the group a small donation, and, in turn, I receive their annual newsletter. It's a simple one-page update on what the Shickley Foundation is doing in the community.

The most recent newsletter shows just how far one small—but determined—town can go to create a bright future: "To date, over $295,000 in grants have been awarded. Another $60,000 will be disbursed next year. Our goal is to have an endowment fund balance (including expectancies) of $8,000,000 by the end of 2020. Together this goal is very achievable. No donation is too small to make a difference."

Let that sink in. A town of about 300 people will soon have an endowment of $8 million. They are already awarding $60,000 per year in grants—and that number will keep growing every year, forever. It's all because their small town got busy sharing their vision.

The funds have been used to renovate the town park and baseball fields in Shickley. They installed welcome signs, including a new electronic sign. A new greenhouse was built at the school to teach horticulture.

Building the Community "Savings" Account

There's a reason why I begin a chapter on strong economies with the story about Shickley's endowment. Just as an individual should always have some savings in case of an emergency, a community should have resources it can use in times of need.

On several occasions, I have visited with communities that have a large project in front of them or are applying for a large grant but are required to have matching funds to submit the proposal. When your community doesn't have a source of income, such as an endowment, it must start from scratch.

For a town such as Shickley, they have a source of funds through an endowment when they need to apply for a grant and must come up with $10,000 on their own.

This source can take many forms. Take Chillicothe, Missouri, a town of just over 10,000 people, for example. It's known as the birthplace of sliced bread. In July 1928, a newspaper headline declared: "Sliced Bread is Made Here. Chillicothe Baking Co., the First Bakers in the World to Sell This Product to the Public."

Chillicothe, Missouri, is the "Home of Sliced Bread." Murals in town tout the city's claim to fame. The town's 19 family foundations are also quite impressive and have allowed Chillicothe to move forward with many local projects.

Perhaps the next best thing to sliced bread are the family foundations. Chillicothe can trace some of its foundations back to the 1940s and 1950s, but lifelong resident Ed Turner says as late as the 1980s there were only two foundations serving the city and county.

Turner recalls a meeting in 1989 called by fellow resident and community leader Ed Douglas. Douglas had spent more than three decades with Citizens Bank, the last 20 years of that tenure as president and CEO. Douglas asked some of the past presidents of the Chamber of Commerce and other local leaders, nine in all, to come to his back porch to visit about the future of the city and county.

"I think we all went into that meeting with some skepticism," Turner said. But he did attend, as Douglas assured them it would last only two hours. Long story short, they left his back porch about 2:30 in the morning.

The group came up with several ideas they thought the community should set as goals. For instance, they could use a YMCA, an 18-hole golf course, and an aquatic center.

Beginning a YMCA was one of the first initiatives they addressed, but the town leaders were originally told the community and county didn't have the population to support it. After more discussion, the YMCA decided to offer Chillicothe an opportunity, with a couple of major caveats. "They asked us to put together a storefront YMCA," Turner said. "We, in turn, would use the schools, churches, and other locations to host the activities." The "storefront" would house offices only. Activities would take place in rented or donated facilities.

That seemed doable. However, the town would need to hire a full-time YMCA professional to oversee the operation and raise $150,000 in six months to move forward.

Turner, Douglas, and the others knew it was a challenge, but one they could meet. "Within six weeks, we had raised $150,000 and hired a full-time professional," Turner said.

It begs the question, "How do you raise $150,000 in six weeks, let alone six months?" It's amazing what a shared vision coupled with a leadership team that's not afraid to knock on doors in the community can accomplish.

After 18 months, they decided it was best to build a YMCA facility so they could continue to grow and not have to rely on public buildings, churches, and parks to host events. It would take $3 million.

Turner remembers one particular luncheon meeting that proved important to the growth of the town, not just the YMCA project. "We called all of the attorneys and accountants together and asked them to support the project," he said.

During that meeting, Turner recalled one local lawyer who stood up and said, "What needs to happen with a lot of these people with a lot of 'rocks in their pockets' is we need to be helping them form some foundations." The statement was not one of jealousy or derision. It was simply an acknowledgment there was wealth in the community and someone needed to share the vision.

As a result, five foundations were formed in support of the YMCA. "People could see what philanthropy could do for a community," Turner said.

Today, there are 19 local family foundations, a community foundation, a hospital foundation, and a foundation to support the public schools. The increase in local philanthropy flourished when the YMCA project began and the community saw it was possible to make their goals a reality.

"Momentum is a big, big factor," Turner said. "The mental attitude of a community is a huge factor. When you prove to people you have a vision and it comes to fruition, they get thinking very positively about what can happen."

One of the foundations was started by a businessman who was selling his farmland and business and wanted the proceeds to benefit local interests. He then convinced one of his farmer friends to also form a foundation. Turner noted most of the 19 family foundations in Chillicothe have more than $1 million in assets. Federal law says 5% of a foundation's corpus must be spent each year. Do the math and that's a sizeable amount of money that goes back into the community every single year.

According to Turner, there are three important words to keep in mind when organizing community efforts: coordination, cooperation, and communication. "If the three Cs are working, you can get a lot of things done," he said.

In addition to funding numerous local projects, the foundations have also helped develop incentive packages to boost economic growth by encouraging businesses to relocate or establish operations in town.

"It makes the bond issue a lot easier to pass because you know the foundations are going to be a player in helping the effort," Turner said. The foundations have eased the tax burden. For example, a large agri-sciences center and county fairgrounds were built using funds provided by the local foundations. In other towns, it would have required a school bond, a local tax increase, or other public monies.

In summary, Turner said: "You've got to identify your resources and motivate those resources to be a part of the community. You need to represent all parts of your community—seniors, youth, ministers, bankers . . . all of them. You've got to have people who can work together really well. You can't have a rotten apple in the barrel because that slows everybody down. If they can work as a cohesive group and not go off as lone rangers, you don't have to be as big as we were—you can do small things and build on that momentum."

The stories of Shickley and Chillicothe help us realize two important points: first, there is often wealth locally and, second, wealth will leave if people don't have a vision and share their story.

Once I was visiting with a regional manager for a bank in a rural area. He had been in the banking business since the early 1980s, primarily working in towns with fewer than 10,000 people. He mentioned to me the first bank he ever worked at, in a small town of about 2,000 people, had lost a significant amount of its deposits over the years.

As we visited more about the subject, it was quickly apparent the bank was not losing its deposits to a neighboring competitor. The money was leaving the area. He said to me: "I was just reading an article in the *American Bankers Association Journal* that said rural small banks lost 7.5% of their deposits in the last five years. If that's consistent with the previous 15 years, then that bank has lost about 30% of its deposits in the last two decades."

"Something else is happening too," he noted. "The number of banks in smaller communities is going down. Many small towns that had a bank 20 years ago don't have one today. Maybe some of the larger, regional hub towns have the same number of banks, but the small towns either lost their bank or only have a small branch bank that's open part time."

An article from the National Center for Business Journalism at Arizona State University supports what that local banker had been seeing. "Community banking's share of domestic deposits has fallen continuously from 40.4% in 2000 to 21.7% in 2014. In 14 years, local banks have lost nearly half of their share of deposits to large banks." As a result, it's difficult for the local banks to continue nurturing the local businesses.

Intent to further illustrate what was happening in the communities around him, the rural banker shared another article from "Insight Vault" by Cornerstone Advisors. The article stated, "According to the FDIC, deposits at fiscal institutions with less than $10 billion in assets declined by roughly 1% in the year ending September 30, 2017, while $10 billion-plus banks grew deposits by 4.5%."

Deposits were leaving those small banks for several reasons, including the rise of peer-to-peer platforms and an increasing amount of cash in health savings accounts held in larger banks. But something else was happening too. "The more important of the two reasons (the first being the aforementioned deposit displacement) why community bank deposit growth isn't keeping up is demographics: Community banks have done a horrible job over the past few years of attracting millennials as checking account customers."

In fact, research shows, "Nearly six in 10 millennials have their primary checking account with a megabank, 17% with a large regional bank, 13% are with a credit union and just 6% are with community banks."

What the banker in Shickley, Nebraska, was seeing in his town was happening nationally—money was leaving small towns and not coming back. When younger generations don't have a connection to their hometown bank and, more importantly, someone they know and trust at that local bank, it's easier to move their money elsewhere and not support the businesses and organizations where the profits were made.

Let me stop for a moment and share a story to illustrate this critical point. When my grandmother passed away in 2015, her funeral was held in a town with fewer than 1,000 people. Due to my mom's family roots, we banked in that small town.

That small-town bank had other branches in the area, and over time, the man I considered "our banker" moved to another branch office about an hour away. He was our lender and a trusted adviser. I could call him to ask a question or advice. He would always promptly return my call.

En route from the funeral home to the cemetery, we passed the bank where we had done business for so many years. Standing on the sidewalk in front of the bank was "our banker." He had driven over an hour to attend the funeral. We had not seen him in the crowd at the funeral home, but he was there.

That's the influence a small-town bank and banker can have in a community. Interestingly, that same banker recently helped a farmer set up an endowment that generates more than $100,000 per year for local projects. Local banks and bankers play an important role in building small towns and rural communities because of the support, advice, and direction they can provide.

Economic resources are necessary to finance plans and goals, but vision is equally important. That said, if a community doesn't have jobs, it will not be able to grow. As one regional economic planner told me, "Ultimately, people leave because they can't make a living where they live." Yes, other factors make a difference, but at the most basic level, an individual and family must have a way to make a living.

Such was the problem facing the town of Calico Rock, Arkansas, population just over 1,500 people. Steven Mitchell is a lifelong resident of the area.

"Back in the 1960s and '70s, all of the buildings had businesses in them," said Steven as he surveyed the 20 or so storefronts on the town's main street along the White River. The place has long been a haven for fisherman to enjoy the scenic waters of the northern part of the Natural State.

But the 1980s and '90s were hard on Calico Rock, as they were for many small towns. By 2000, there was only one business operating on main street. All the other 20 or so stores were closed.

You might remember I said a total town makeover requires people recognizing the need. Not everyone will see the need, mind you. Heck, my grandfather was selling electricity, and not everyone saw the need for it. You just need "some" people to see the need.

Let me pause for a moment and quantify "some." The University of Quebec did a study to examine how major changes move through organizations, including how many people need to be committed for those changes to take place.

The study concluded it takes the square root of the total number of people in the group for change to move through an organization. In other words, if you have a group of 100 people, it takes 10 committed people to influence change.

Back to Calico Rock. People could see the storefronts were vacant and buildings were in disrepair. However, some groups felt they couldn't change the trend. Others didn't think they could or should raise money to try to save the downtown.

Eventually, the local museum's board of directors decided to do something. When I say "museum," we aren't talking about the Smithsonian staff. This is a group of volunteers who were determined to make some changes.

They saw the need and decided they could effectively lead change in Calico Rock. "It's a slow process, and that's something people have to be aware of from the beginning," Steven cautioned. "It doesn't just happen overnight."

The museum's board of directors developed a unique plan to fill storefronts and create jobs in Calico Rock. "For us, we focused on the arts and creative economy. We got together local artists who had a skill but not necessarily an outlet to sell their work," Steven explained.

Calico Rock, Arkansas, was down to its last business on Main Street. The local museum board raised funds to buy a building and put a business in it. Today, they own seven buildings, and only two storefronts are unoccupied.

The next step took some courage and a lot of hard work. "We bought a building using a loan from our local community bank," Steven said. "We had to raise donations. Sometimes we did that by having a concert in the park and asking for $2 donations." The museum's board of directors was able to purchase a beautiful stone building that needed some restoration on the corner of the block.

They used the second story and some of the basement for museum exhibits. The main floor was divided into "booths," which local artisans could rent to sell their wares. Eventually, the museum board decided not to charge rent but instead receive a percentage of the sales. In addition, those who had booths agreed to volunteer to staff the museum at least one day per month.

The museum board not only paid off the building but also were inspired to purchase more buildings, which now numbers seven. They reopened a café. They opened an art gallery and put a children's science center in the basement using displays from a larger museum in Little Rock that needed to rotate its exhibits.

"As far as the operations and other staffing are concerned, we are totally self-sufficient," Steven said. "The city of Calico Rock has seen a $4,000 to $5,000 increase every month in their sales tax collection."

Think of the difference several thousand *extra* dollars per month makes in a city's budget. It was mostly because an unlikely group, the local museum board, saw the vision and began reviving storefronts where businesses could flourish. Now, with artisans, an art gallery, a science center, a café, and much more, the little town has something for the entire family.

If you've heard of Hamilton, Missouri, it's perhaps for a successful businessman who was born there in 1875. James Cash Penney graduated from the local high school and established the chain of stores that bears his name. He opened his five-hundredth store in his hometown of Hamilton in the 1920s. Penney waited that long to come to his hometown out of respect to the local merchant who helped him learn the business. When his mentor retired, Penney bought the store and reopened it under his J.C. Penney brand.

But Hamilton suffered the economic woes of the 1980s farm crisis like many other small towns. In 1981, the J.C. Penney store in Hamilton closed. Penney had died a decade earlier. If he were alive, locals claimed, Penney would have never let the hometown store close.

In 1981, the *New York Times* wrote of the Hamilton store closing: "The J.C. Penney legend still thrives in Hamilton—but only through the Penney High School and the $250,000 library and museum Mr. Penney's family and company helped build."

Interestingly, the business that resides in the old J.C. Penney store today is part of the town's economic makeover. "Missouri Star Quilt began here in about 2008," says Alan Drake, Hamilton's city manager. "Since then they've grown to employ over 250 people." That's an amazing number of jobs when you consider Hamilton's population is only 1,809.

Some have called the town the "Disneyland of Quilting." In fact, Missouri Star Quilt Company owns 11 stores on the town's main street, each with its own theme. Let that sink in for a second. A town that in the early 2000s had no quilt stores and no tie to the pastime now has *11* such stores on a three-block-long main street.

Hamilton, Missouri, was the boyhood home of J.C. Penney. He opened his five-hundredth store in his old hometown in the 1920s. That store closed in the 1980s. Today, it is occupied by one of about a dozen quilt stores in the small town that have been a vital link to economic revitalization.

In the summer it can be hard to find a parking place on the streets. It's common for bus tours to stop in Hamilton. "People from all over the world come here," Alan explained. The founders of the company do a great job of connecting to people online through video tutorials. Thousands of people visit Hamilton for special events and to learn the craft of quilting.

Before the quilting revival hit Hamilton, Alan said a lot of businesses were leaving town. "The town was like a lot of towns in northwest Missouri. It was losing a lot of educated people going elsewhere to find good jobs," he explained.

The quilt shops bring an estimated 6,000 to 8,000 additional people to Hamilton each month. Not every visitor is a quilter, but people need a place to eat, sleep, and fuel up with gas and snacks for a road trip. As a result, other businesses have opened in Hamilton as well. Walk into the Blue Sage restaurant on main street and you'd think you were in a high-end establishment in a big city.

Sometimes the economic vitality of a small town does revolve around one type of business, such as quilting in Hamilton, or one specific business. Consider the fortunes of Wall, South Dakota. If you've heard of the town, it's mostly likely because you know, or have stopped at, the biggest business in that town of 766 people—Wall Drug.

But many people don't know the story of Wall Drug and how the business and the town could have slowly dwindled away.

Ted and Dorothy Hustead came to Wall in the early 1930s. Ted had just graduated top of his class from pharmacy school at the University of Nebraska. For the first five years, the tiny drug store struggled to make ends meet.

One hot summer day, Dorothy began to think of all the cars traveling the hot, dusty road out of the nearby Badlands National Park. She thought to herself, "Here we sit with all of the ice in world for this soda fountain, yet we have no customers."

She had an idea to put up a sign advertising free ice water at the Hustead Drug Store. Ted thought the idea was a little corny but nonetheless sent two boys to paint and erect a small sign. Before the pair could return to the store, the first car pulled in to get their free ice water.

If one sign had such a great impact, Ted thought more signs would bring even more customers. It began a tradition that continues across Interstate 90 with dozens of Wall Drug signs stretching from Minnesota to Wyoming.

Wall Drug wouldn't be the 76,000-square-foot store it is today if not for Ted and Dorothy's son Bill. When he was at boarding school, people would ask him where he was from. When he said, "Wall," they would often respond, "That's the town with the tiny drugstore with all of the signs."

Bill vowed that if he returned to the family business, he would create a place worthy of the advertising boards that stretched hundreds of miles in both directions. Today, Bill's son Rick oversees the operation. "He built our dining rooms; he built our western shopping mall," Rick said, plus much, much more. "We see on a peak day 20,000 people."

Wall Drug has had signs on the docks in Amsterdam, on London's double-decker busses, and in the subways of Paris—all pointing people to a store that still offers free ice water and free coffee and donuts to veterans.

In fact, Rick says when he came back home to the family business in 1981, the first thing his dad had him do was learn to make donuts. His dad has only one rule: "We never run out of donuts," Rick said.

A town's economic makeover could come from existing businesses, such as the case for Wall Drug, or it might be spurred by new businesses, such as the Missouri Star Quilt Company or the storefronts developed in Calico Rock.

While we might believe rural economies lag those of larger metro areas, there's an interesting fact when it comes to business start-ups in rural areas. Research published in *U.S. News and World Report* found rural counties with fewer than 2,500 residents that aren't adjacent to a metro area have a rate of 234 self-employed business owners per 1,000 residents. That's the highest rate among locations surveyed. If those counties with fewer than 2,500 residents are adjacent to a metro area, the rate dips to 177 per 1,000.

However, when compared with metro areas of all sizes, from fewer than 250,000 people to more than one million citizens, the rate of self-employed businessowners averages about 125 per 1,000. So, the smallest of counties have an entrepreneurship rate about twice that of the metro areas.

Some might say the rate is significantly higher in rural areas due to the number of self-employed farmers. However, researchers who authored the study note farmers make up only one-sixth of business owners in those most rural counties.

Interestingly, the survival rate of those self-employed businesses is also higher in the rural counties. In counties with fewer than 2,500 residents, 71.6% of self-employed businesses survive. As counties increase in size, the survival rate continues to decrease. The lowest survival rate is in metro areas of more than one million people, where the mark stands at 66.5%.

Rural areas and small towns have an entrepreneurial spirit. They often have people with the know-how and work ethic to create the total town makeover. From my experience, the town's overall success is determined by how well those independent and small-business owners work together to promote and build the town around them.

There is nothing wrong with small towns and cities actively recruiting businesses. However, it's often difficult for small towns to do this because they lack the transportation, infrastructure, and technology base companies require.

I've found for many communities, the best, and often underutilized, method to develop businesses is to do so from within. The goal is to grow businesses from those who already live there. Statistics point to the fact that less populated counties already have people willing to start those businesses. The goal is to help them thrive.

Troy Bancroft's father-in-law began AgroLiquid fertilizer company in 1983. Farmers were looking for different types of crop nutrients and application methods, especially in Michigan's fruit orchards. Bancroft's company provided new and innovative products that could improve the nutrition of trees and plants, producing more bountiful crops while remaining safe for the environment.

Over time, the company began to grow at a rural crossroads just outside of St. Johns, Michigan, a town of about 8,000 residents. Interestingly, when the company recently decided to build a new headquarters, the family owners placed the building at the same corner where they'd been for more than 30 years.

"Why did we choose here?" Troy asked, repeating the question I had just queried him. "Well, we'd been at this corner since 1985. It was home to us."

This is no small building, mind you. It's just under 60,000 square feet with about 40 employees on site. The company would have to invest in infrastructure to make it happen due to the rural location.

"I said to my boys, 'When we build this building, it's going to be a branded building in a rural area,'" Troy explained. The family knew they had to be in this for the long haul, but they were committed to their roots.

"It was important for us to make a difference in our community and to put something back from which we had drawn so much for so long," Troy said. And that's where this story really speaks to the total town makeover. The *economic* makeover in small-town America is often about much more than *just* a business. It's about the relationship between the business owner and the community and what both gain as a result.

The first time I met Troy at his headquarters, he mentioned something about outside groups using their conference rooms. "There's seven to 10 events here each week that are not our events," he explained. In fact, his senior management team recently had to meet in the kitchenette because all the rooms were being used by outside groups.

"But that didn't make me feel bad," Troy chuckled. "I felt good knowing other people were making good use of the rooms as well. It's very gratifying to help the community." The conference rooms can seat 150 people, and they have the latest technology. It's a great asset for a small town, and the rooms can be used by local groups free of charge.

Troy has hosted the high school prom at their headquarters, and he brought in his Model A for couples to have a unique backdrop for their pictures. One of the things that impressed me about the AgroLiquid story is that their new headquarters—and their business, for that matter—is about much more than "business." It's about helping to build their community and their industry for generations to come. The Bancroft family's commitment to their community runs deep.

The new 60,000-square-foot headquarters of AgroLiquid Fertilizers in St. Johns, Michigan, includes the IQhub, an interactive agricultural museum. AgroLiquid not only chose to build their new headquarters in their hometown but also allow the community to use their conference rooms free of charge. *Photo courtesy AgroLiquid Fertilizers*

One wing of their headquarters is called the "IQhub." You might think of it as an interactive agricultural museum and learning center. You can learn about the history of agriculture as well as have fun experiencing what life is like tilling the land today.

"As people come to our building, they are sometimes, quite frankly, in awe. But I don't want to be known as the guy with the big building," Troy said. "I would like to be known as the guy who took the time to explain the importance of agriculture."

All too often, small towns dismiss their ability to grow their own "Troy Bancroft" in their own backyard. I recently sat in on a planning meeting for a small town in which the topic of their economy was up for discussion. Several people mentioned, "We need to bring businesses here!" There's certainly nothing wrong with attracting new businesses, but the problem is we often overlook the opportunities with people who already call the community home. One of the first steps in a total town makeover is to start looking at the businesses (and potential business owners) within the existing community and see how you can help them thrive. After all, they're already located in your community.

I had a chance to sit down with Deb Markley, the cofounder for the Center for Rural Entrepreneurship. Much of her life has been devoted to the topics in this chapter as she crisscrosses the country helping towns see the economic opportunities they might possess.

One of the first questions she asks when sitting down with community leaders is, "Who are the people we have here who are trying to start and grow new businesses, and what resources do we have to support them?" She then turns the table and has those towns ask, "What assets are we not using very well?" It could be empty buildings on Main Street that could be turned into places for entrepreneurs. Perhaps the city has a lake or riverfront that offers opportunities. "There is asset mapping that has to be done with an entrepreneur in mind," Markley said.

For instance, part of the process is helping small towns see the barriers to new businesses. "You're not going to attract a young new entrepreneur if you don't have access to broadband," she says.

It takes shared input within a community. "Part of what rural communities are increasingly doing better than they have in the past is working across 'silos,' having economic development sit down with the education system, and having the nonprofit sector sit down with the business community," she explains. "For gains to be made, people have to reach across those lines to see how everyone can work toward a common goal. Those critical issues cannot be effectively dealt with by a single entity or individual."

It takes leaders willing to reach across imaginary lines and look for the opportunities for economic growth. Ron Drake, from Siloam Springs, Arkansas, is one of those individuals who helps small towns see the opportunities. Much of his work is helping people see the vision for what a building could be. It's something Ron does every day.

"We have a mission of restoring neighborhoods one house at a time," Ron said. "We buy one or two houses in one block and restore them." He would also encourage other nearby property owners to paint and renovate their homes. "We are seeing property values in an entire neighborhood elevate," he said.

As I mentioned in the previous chapter, though, Ron found "flipping" buildings to be a much bigger challenge than flipping homes. Financing was more difficult. It often requires forming partnerships with others in the community who share the vision of what a building could be and in such a way a tenant would open a business inside the new space.

Ron wrote a book, *Flip This Town*, which shares his challenges and successes and provides a road map for small-town redevelopment. "There's not very many people helping small towns," Ron said. "It's easy to find consultants and architects who will work in Fayetteville and Little Rock, but to try to find someone who will help a town of 3,000 people is tough." That's why Ron wrote the book and devotes his time to working in small towns.

"I believe there are people in every community with the ability to do great things. It's inspiring them, convincing them, and showing them the numbers work," Ron said. "Downtown restoration is not bricks and mortar—it's the restoration of the mind and believing it's possible in your town."

There's a highway bypass around Siloam Springs that features chain restaurants and big-box stores. If you venture into the historic downtown area, you'll see the once-closed storefronts are now like new, housing new businesses and apartments thanks to Ron and others who helped bring life back into Siloam Springs.

"The best way to bring life downtown is to bring lives downtown," Ron said. He often encourages people in small towns to look up—both figuratively and literally. Many older buildings in small towns are two stories, which allowed the business owner to live above his or her store.

Over time most of those second-story rooms were abandoned as families no longer wanted to live in a tight space directly above their business. "Nobody thought residential would work in downtown Siloam Springs because it's too small and there's nothing to do," Ron said, repeating all the reasons he was told his idea wouldn't work. However, Ron has found those second-story areas are perfect to renovate into apartments and studios. There have been challenges, but the residential space has been a great addition to the downtown makeover.

Ron has good advice for those old storefronts. "Clean up the buildings and remove the ugly sheet metal facades," he said, "and realize the downtown, no matter how large or small, in your town is vital. Every artery of the community comes from the downtown. So, if your downtown's not healthy, if your heart is not healthy, your town is not healthy."

So how do small towns and rural America help develop strong economies? As you've read, there are several ways to make positives steps, but, in general, consider the following goals to pull off a total town makeover:

- Does your community have a permanent source of seed money, through endowments or local foundations, that can be a tool to begin projects or provide the matching funds for grants?
- What businesses would sprout in your area if they had the resources to do so? Calico Rock, Arkansas, had several skilled artisans, but they lacked a place to sell their wares because no single person could generate the means to do so. Yet, when provided a small shared space, those same artisans could turn a profit and sustain a building.
- Is there a particular "industry" that is a natural fit for your area? For Hamilton, Missouri, quilting jump-started the economy.

Some small towns have become meccas for antique stores. Others have found food and restaurants to be an attraction. Maybe it's Western sports, classic tractors, and cars. Is there a "theme" your town can run with to help build businesses?

- Do not neglect the opportunities to build businesses from within. AgroLiquid could have built a headquarters almost anywhere in the United States—but they chose their hometown. Small towns already show a propensity for small-business start-ups, so help foster the growth of young people with ideas. After all, that's what the Bancroft family did.

- Ultimately, one of the biggest challenges to economic growth is what Ron Drake mentioned: "restoration of the mind." It might sound cliché, but you need to believe you can do it. Many small towns never advance beyond that point. You and I must be the champions to see the vision, share the vision, and help it come true.

CHAPTER 3
Vibrant Communities

A few years ago, I was driving from Salt Lake City to western Colorado to conduct interviews for our *American Countryside* broadcasts. I stopped in Vernal, Utah, to find out more about a brick bank building in town. It might not sound that unusual, until you learn the backstory.

The construction process for the bank started in 1916. The bricks the bank president picked out for the front of the building had to be shipped 427 miles by wagon from Salt Lake City. However, the shipping cost could be cut in half if the bricks were sent via the U.S. Postal Service in 50-pound bundles.

The first shipment of bricks was accompanied by the bank president himself. The large haul caused the train to run a half hour behind schedule after stopping to unload the bricks.

The post office soon realized shipping 80,000 bricks via parcel post was a big problem. As a result, they instituted new rules: a limit of 200 pounds a day per consignor to a specific address. The announcement of the rule change stated: "It is not the intent of the U.S. Postal Service that buildings be shipped through the mail." The bank in Vernal still stands— all 80,000 bricks delivered via parcel post.

It's a great story from a small town, but my visit to Vernal also produced an unexpected find. As I drove through the city of 9,200, I saw large hanging baskets overflowing with vibrant, beautiful flowers hanging from the street lamps.

It all began with a Chamber of Commerce committee member who helped purchase and plant the flowers. Now the city parks department carries on the tradition with a mission to keep Vernal "a beautiful place to live." Residents can sign up to help plant the flowers, which takes place each May. These days, the city boasts more than 1,500 planters and hanging baskets.

Seeing all the flowers as you drive through Vernal gives the impression this must be a great place to live. The small town takes a lot of pride in its appearance—and the flowers literally make the streets come alive.

What do your home and community "say" to others when they arrive? In addition to economic prosperity, the "vibrancy" of a community influences the ability of a total makeover.

What is "vibrancy"? Perhaps it's all the factors that influence a person to make a home in a specific place. There is a difference between a house and a home. Communities must set about the work of creating a place that is "home."

In chapter 2, I talked about Shickley, Nebraska's, amazing endowment that's expected to grow beyond $8 million. It's interesting that some of the first projects the endowment funded helped create a more vibrant community. When they built a new city hall, they included space for a community fitness facility complete with the latest equipment. There was a need for such a facility, which added "vibrancy" to Shickley.

Charles City, Iowa, has just under 8,000 residents. In 2011, the town, which straddles the Charles River, created a white-water recreation area. It's the only white-water area in the entire state. Not only can you kayak, paddleboard, and tube down the course but also there's a beautiful path to walk along the river's edge.

In my travels, I often ask communities one simple question: "What can you find here that is difficult to find anywhere else?"

The numerous and enormous flower baskets in Vernal set it apart from other towns. The white-water course in Charles City is one-of-a-kind in the state. There are plenty of fitness centers in the nation, but it would be hard to find one as new and well stocked as the one in Shickley.

The answer to my question could be a unique historical attraction or an event. The answer could very well be something that's commonplace or "out-of-place" to local residents.

Here's why it's so important to have a good answer when asked what makes your community special: people often want to be part of something others don't have. That's what gives your community a sense of pride. It's what sets you apart.

The Questions to Ask

Have you ever encountered someone who snidely remarked, "What makes you so special?" Of course, that question isn't meant to be answered, but rather intended to be the put-down that moves you to your proper place in line.

However, when it comes to a total town makeover, it's one of the most important questions to ask. What makes your community special? What makes your town stand out from the rest? In fact, what can be found only in your town and nowhere else?

It's important to be specific and unique. Almost everyone will say, "We have nice people, the quality of life is good, and it's a peaceful place to live." That's true for most small towns and rural America. But what makes you so special? The places that have successfully answered that question have found it to be a catalyst for a total town makeover.

The answer to this question can come in many forms. Sometimes the answer is rooted deep in history. In other cases, the town "invents" its special place in the world. There are several ways a town can go about distinguishing itself.

I've found three ways communities effectively answer the question of what makes them special. Those ways are:

- Develop something from nothing. Create your own special "something" about your community.
- Reinvigorate something that once set the community apart.
- Grow something you already have in the community.

Maybe the best way to ask this question is simply, "What's painted on your water tower?" Drive into Faulkton, South Dakota (population 736), and you'll find its claim to fame painted on the city water tower. The story behind the moniker shows how one person can help answer the question, "What makes your place special?"

Bob Ketterling grew up in the Depression years of the 1930s. As a child, he always wanted to ride a merry-go-round; however, his family could rarely afford to pay the few cents for the ride. Bob's childhood dream never left him as the years passed, but he kept his idea a secret, even from his wife, Loretta.

Without her knowledge, Bob and a friend went to an auction in Rapid City and bought a 1925 C.W. Parker Carousel. The 20 horses and two benches were just a pile of pieces that needed to be restored and reconstructed if any child was to ever ride them again.

"He set it up in our backyard to start off with," said Loretta when we sat down to visit in a park. "It was all dismantled, and pieces were missing." She really didn't know what to think of her husband's new hobby, but slowly and surely, he worked to put the antique back together.

"I was at work, and when I came home, the yard was full of people," Loretta remembers of the day her husband finally got the carousel operational. They quickly decided the backyard was not the place to operate the machine, so they set it up across the street from the courthouse.

Bob never charged an admission fee and rarely took donations. It was his gift to the town and the families of the area. Bob passed away in 1988. Just before his death, local leaders decided to honor Bob by crowning Faulkton as "The Carousel City." Those are the words painted on the town's water tower.

Loretta still assists with the carousel, along with resident Bob Becker, who operates the ride three days each week. When I visited, Bob showed me the amusement ride and even let me take several spins. "I wouldn't be surprised if some kids hear the ride running and come up here," he said.

Sure enough, they came. First, a car stopped with two young boys. Then a girl rode up the street on her bicycle to take a ride. Bob told me there are times when all 20 horses have riders and there's a line of kids waiting for their turn.

Bob never set out to make his town "The Carousel City." He was a humble man who simply wanted to share a gift with his community. One man's time and gift made this community a place that is special.

Loretta Ketterling (pictured) was surprised when her husband, Bob, purchased a vintage carousel and brought it to their home of Faulkton, South Dakota. Today, the carousel sits under cover and is operated several times each week, free of charge, for young and old to ride. The city repainted its water tower to proclaim the town "The Carousel City," in honor of Bob.

I drove about two hours northeast of Faulkton to the even smaller town of Roslyn (population 183). Lawrence Diggs came to Roslyn from San Francisco in the 1990s. Some of the locals told me Lawrence could have felt out of place in their small town, but that wasn't the case. Lawrence is African American, and at the time, had a large Afro. It's safe to say he stood out in the small farming community.

He decided to purchase a home, and while visiting with a new neighbor, the man gave Lawrence his truck keys and said he was welcome to use the truck anytime. It was a case of small-town hospitality—and it helped hook Lawrence on making it his home.

I talked with Richard Snaza, a local farmer, who remembers Lawrence's arrival in Roslyn. "He could see things were really not happening in town, and he said, 'You need something to attract people here.'"

So, townspeople began to discuss what might bring visitors to a town of 183 people that is well off the biggest of highways. "Different people had different ideas, but his idea was vinegar," Richard recalls.

Yes, vinegar. Lawrence had become interested in vinegar while in California and had researched the product he used when preparing meals. In fact, Lawrence proposed launching the International Vinegar Museum—and that's just what happened in 1999.

You can proclaim yourself the "international" vinegar museum when there are no others. The idea was no joke, though. Locals renovated the interior of an old school gym, and they began creating displays about vinegar.

Roslyn, South Dakota, is home to the International Vinegar Museum. These displays were created inside the old schoolhouse in town. The museum hosts annual events and a vinegar festival. Not only does the museum attract visitors but also some tourists have decided to buy homes and property in the area after their visit here.

People took notice. Richard volunteers at the museum and says they get visitors from across the nation and many foreign countries. The museum sells different types of vinegar, and the sales more than offset the cost of operating the museum.

"We have what we call our Vinegar Festival. We have a parade, a vinegar queen, and entertainment," Richard explained. Lawrence and others hold cooking demonstrations with vinegar.

But Richard also shared the larger, long-term impact on the town. "The museum has attracted people to town to look around," he said. There's a lot of hunting and fishing opportunities in the area. Some people have bought a house to live in during hunting season, while others have purchased a property as a full-time residence. "We've attracted people into town, and we hope we can keep doing it," Richard said.

Roslyn is a good example of a community that developed their own "specialness" from scratch. Other communities have accomplished similar feats. In the 1960s, the Spivey's Corner, North Carolina, volunteer fire department began the National Hollerin' Contest. The contest was a way to raise money for the organization and to keep alive the traditional "hollers" farmers used to communicate from farm to farm.

Winners of the contest have appeared on late-night talk shows. Spivey's Corner found what made them special by reviving a folk art that helped people learn and laugh along with their local history.

The volunteer fire department did quite well too! They were able to purchase more modern equipment and a better facility to house that equipment. The Hollerin' Contest made Spivey's Corner special, and it allowed community resources to grow. As a result, it's a more vibrant community.

In recent years, it has become challenging to continue to hold the contest as leadership ages and times change. We will discuss some of these challenges and possible solutions in chapter 5. However, just because the Hollerin' Contest neared its fiftieth anniversary doesn't mean it's obsolete. In fact, some communities are finding their "vibrancy" by reinvigorating the old.

Take Red Cloud, Nebraska, for instance. Red Cloud's claim to fame is the home of Pulitzer Prize–winning author Willa Cather. Born in 1873, Cather lived her teenage and early adult years in the small town on the south-central Nebraska prairie.

Maybe you've heard of her. As years have passed, though, more people have not. Her novels are still some of the best in American literature, but the town found it a challenge to keep Cather's name and work top-of-mind since her passing in 1947.

Ashley Olson is the director of the Willa Cather Foundation. We sat down to talk in the Cather Visitors Center on the town's main street. "I think our organization has done a lot of work in recent years to make sure Cather is able to maintain that status as a great American novelist," she explained. The town has always honored the hometown writer, but over time, the girlhood home could have faded.

How did Red Cloud reinvigorate the Cather story? It took the work of several organizations coming together and providing additional opportunities beyond the historic Cather home tour. "We try to share Cather with the world through other mediums. We have a performing arts center at the Red Cloud Opera House," Ashley said. The opera house is the second story of the visitors center. The century-old building has been beautifully restored.

Many small towns across America had such opera houses. Some of those venues occupied an entire building, while others used the upstairs of a building as in Red Cloud. In fact, that opera house is were Cather's high school graduation was held.

Red Cloud brought the Opera House back to life. Productions of Cather's work can be seen there, as well as other theatrical events. It has become a draw for those wanting to connect with the arts.

"Now we have all of this extended programming beyond the historic site tours," Ashley said. "We have artists' signings, lectures, and gallery exhibits. We have a 612-acre native prairie south of Red Cloud that we use for programming and is open year-round," she added.

Creating a vibrant community connected to the Pulitzer Prize-winning author has made this small town in south-central Nebraska a destination. For some it has become a new home. "With all the technological advances we've had for a lot of positions, people can choose to live and work wherever they desire," Ashley said. "We've really tried to work to make Red Cloud an attractive place."

It's important to note what makes Red Cloud "special" and unique from other towns is its connection to Willa Cather. The community would perhaps always have a childhood home people could tour. However, if they did nothing else, that site would simply become a place that drew a handful of tourists each year. It's the programming, opportunities, and businesses that have been built around the link to Cather that are important.

This process can take time, but it can generate exponential results as others in the community see the success that's being generated. When citizens and businessowners see building renovations and a new visitors center open (in the case of Red Cloud), they are inspired to make positive changes as well.

It's also worth noting Red Cloud does more than simply promote the physical places linked to Cather. They have developed a list of activities for locals and visitors to take part in year-round. This draws people to the area, and in some cases, those people make a home there. That's quite an accomplishment for a town such as Red Cloud that is far from a major metro hub.

Creating Vibrancy

When it comes to building a vibrant community through activities, there's perhaps no place better than Port Townsend, Washington. This town of about 10,000 sits on the western side of Puget Sound. Mari Mullen directs the main street program in Port Townsend. "We have eclectic events," she said. "We have events that don't happen anywhere else."

For instance, one event is called the Steam Punk Festival. "It's the future as if it would have been powered by steam," Mari explained. "People are dressed in very unusual outfits that are Victorian but from another dimension."

A second event is the Kinetic Sculpture Race. "It's basically human-powered vehicles that you create," Mari said. "They need to be able to go on water, go on land, and go through the dismal mud bog out at the fairgrounds."

The town also hosts common events, such as outdoor movie nights, that are quite impressive. The events help build a sense of home for the residents, and they provide a reason for people to pay a visit. The city boasts various restaurants and has found culinary tourism to be a draw, as well.

Perhaps most unique is an annual event Port Townsend hosts every year during the summer. At the event, they publicize the annual Port Townsend "family picture." Everyone is invited to stand in one of the town's intersections while a group photo is taken by a photographer standing atop one of the town's buildings.

Port Townsend, Washington, takes a "family picture" each year and has prints available for purchase. The annual tradition is one that makes this town feel like a close-knit community. *Photo courtesy Port Townsend Main Street Program, Photo by David Conklin, Printed by Printery Communications*

The pictures are printed that day in large poster sizes, and people can take home their "family" portrait. You know you have a vibrant community when hundreds of people turn out annually to take a picture with their fellow citizens.

Organizing a large list of events, and finding the people and resources to do so, can be a challenge for communities. However, those events are often what make communities special. They bring community pride and are the reasons people make a home there. Vibrant communities not only host these special events but also offer permanent recreational opportunities that persuade people to make it their home.

Osage, Iowa, is a town of 3,600 people in north-central Iowa. Mason City, Iowa, a city of just under 30,000, is a half-hour drive. In 2006, Osage's mayor, Steve Cooper, arranged for six local groups to meet and discuss goals for the area.

What resulted was an intergovernmental partnership known as "28E," for the state code that governs it. The city, schools, Osage Education Foundation, city municipal utilities, county historical society, and county agricultural society began work on what is today called the Cedar River Complex. The complex includes a new auditorium capable of hosting top-notch theatrical performances, an aquatic center that includes a lazy river, an indoor fitness center, basketball courts, and a historical museum, to name just some of the amenities.

Robert, a 1943 Osage graduate, and Patricia Kern issued a $5-million challenge grant. The challenge was met, raising additional money for the $18-million complex. Walk into the Cedar River Complex and you would think you've stumbled into a facility for a town many times the size of Osage.

Certainly, the local citizens appreciate it, but what is the larger effect? JR and Lisa Peterson live on a farm outside of Osage. Lisa graduated from the high school in Osage in the late 1990s. She gained national attention when she was elected president of the National FFA Organization. She met her husband, JR, a successful agribusinessman in his own right, through FFA. Both had careers that took them outside of Iowa.

However, today they are back near Lisa's roots. "The Cedar River Complex is a big reason we moved back here," Lisa said. The amenities are similar to those the couple found in large cities where they previously lived. "I met many of my friends I have today there," she said of the complex. Classes are offered for children and adults, and the facility serves as a connecting point for people from neighboring communities.

Osage, Iowa (population: 3,619), raised money to build a very impressive recreation facility, the Cedar River Complex. It includes an indoor swimming pool, a lazy river, basketball courts, an elevated walking track, a theater, and much more. The amenities have attracted families to the community, as they are equal to what could be found in much larger cities.

The most important piece—and what I consider the most difficult challenge—to creating a vibrant community is developing a vibrant personality for the community. How do you create an atmosphere that is welcoming to newcomers? How do you find ways to help people feel connected and involved?

Countless times in my interviews in small towns I've heard people say, "I moved here 35 years ago, and I still feel like I'm an outsider." Such feelings can be a silent, yet very real, barrier to getting newcomers involved in a community. In fact, it's an attitude that might keep potential residents from even making a town their home at all.

One of the first and most important ways to create the right atmosphere is through the local school system. We'll focus on some of those specifics in the next chapter, but the ability of schools to welcome and involve parents in the educational process is an important door to building the community's personality as well.

It Begins with One Person

We should not neglect the fact that one person can play a very important role in building the personality of a place. Nancy Goodwin is a resident of Gays, Illinois, a town of fewer than 300 people. When you drive through town, you might be tempted to take a two-block detour when you see a sign point the way to the two-story outhouse.

It's actually a very rare historical item in our country today. "Back in the 1800s, they had two-story outhouses to accommodate the apartments upstairs," Nancy explained. There was once a general store with second-story apartments. A two-story outhouse allowed those living upstairs not to have to go to the ground level each time they needed to use the toilet.

Of course, a two-story outhouse leaves many with a very important question: What if you're using the lower level of the outhouse and someone decides to use the second level at the same time? Nancy just smiles and says, "That's a secret of the town of Gays." (There's an offset in the wall that prevents the unthinkable from happening).

But what makes this site so unique is Nancy herself. There's a small box next to the outhouse where people can sign their name to a guest registry. They can also sign their name to a card and drop it in a box. Nancy collects the cards several times each week and then writes postcards (with the picture of the outhouse) to those who have stopped to visit the site.

Nancy Goodwin helps oversee the two-story outhouse in Gays, Illinois. The unique piece of history has many people stopping to take pictures of the oddity. If you write your name and address in the guestbook, you may just get a personal note from Nancy thanking you for stopping in their town.

There are even bus tours that stop in Gays! I believe the main reason they stop is because of the positive impression one woman makes in this little town. Nancy exemplifies what it means to go out of your way to welcome others.

Another perfect example of the difference one person can make in a town is a man I met quite by accident in Maryville, Missouri. The impression he made on me has lasted a lifetime. Fred Mares is greeter "extraordinaire" at the Hy-Vee supermarket in Maryville. (Fred has not been able to work at Hy-Vee much lately due to health reasons, but he is still a well-known personality in the community. He was still very active at Hy-Vee when I originally met and interviewed him.) Although he has many other duties beyond just saying "hello" to those who enter the store, his ability to build relationships with customers is what has won the store loyal patrons and made Fred well known to those in his community.

Fred truly defines what it is to do a job well. He goes far beyond a simple smile when someone enters. He begins by introducing himself, and he eventually learns the names of the many people who shop there. He calls people by their first names and takes a sincere interest in their lives. It isn't uncommon for Fred to ask about someone's relative who is ill or about a new grandchild in the family. When people see Fred, he is like another member of the family.

Fred shares that one of his secrets is reading the local newspapers. He looks at birth notices, community awards, events, and even obituaries. He often sends a card of congratulations to his customers when something good happens to them or their family. He has been known to personally travel to a funeral visitation at night just to pay his respects to a customer who has lost a loved one.

One day Fred noticed how many foreign-exchange students from the local university came to Hy-Vee to buy their groceries. These young people, who spoke English as a second language, are often too shy to ask questions. Fred took it upon himself to learn simple phrases in all their native languages. They're often surprised to hear Fred speaking familiar words when they enter the store.

Fred builds relationships by focusing on the needs of others and making them feel at home. He truly cares about more than what groceries they purchase. People are often fascinated to learn he's an accomplished writer and even won a Pulitzer Prize for reporting at the *Kansas City Star*.

Fred says the key to building these relationships is found in the little things. He is sure to say "please" and "thank you" to other employees every time they assist him with something around the store. He knows building lasting relationships is about far more than just saying "hello." It requires the extra effort to truly get to know others and help meet their needs. Little things make a huge difference!

Every community needs several "Freds" in their midst. These are people who go out of their way to welcome everyone—the newcomer as well as the person whose family lineage has roots three generations deep. They are sincere in their desire to see everyone find joy in the place they live, and they take a personal interest in seeing others succeed.

Some towns and cities will go as far as having an official "welcome liaison" who meets new residents, helps them feel at home, and works to get them involved in local events. In some places, this might be an entire committee. It's a great idea that can work with varying degrees of success. It takes the right person/people for the job.

Developing a vibrant personality in a community can't be confined to a one-time meeting between a newcomer and a liaison. It takes a commitment to having a welcoming attitude and a sense of belonging.

Vibrant communities are places where neighbors help neighbors, and there's a synergy that can transform the place for the better. Let me take you to a town in Europe that takes community support to another level. Sienna, Italy, is a city of about 50,000 people. The city is divided into wards called *contradas*. You might think of a contrada as a neighborhood, the origins of which date back centuries.

Today there are 17 contradas in Sienna. While they're not divided in exact equal parts, each contrada has a population of about 3,000 people. Walk the streets of Sienna and you'll see plenty of flags, shields, and emblems, with the colors of the contradas, adorning the walls of homes and buildings. A stroll through the streets might bring you past sea shells, wolves, rams, and more—the symbols of each contrada.

You don't have to spend much time in Sienna to realize the importance of the contrada in people's lives. For instance, you'll find a baptismal fount in each contrada. Once a child is baptized in the church, they are then baptized into the contrada.

There's great pride in the "extended family." In fact, you'll quickly notice the city is very clean. Trash receptacles are easy to find, and even though there are thousands of visitors each year, you'd be pressed to find trash left behind from any of them. Each neighborhood makes sure their "home" looks its best, which means keeping the streets clean.

Many have commented on the lack of crime in the city. No one wants to bring shame on the contrada. There's also an absence of beggars on the street. Everyone in the contrada pitches in to take care of its members. No one should ever be left behind.

One event truly stands out in Sienna. It's called the Palio, a horse race first run in 1656. It's held twice each year on July 2 and August 16. Ten horses, one from each contrada, run a three-lap race around the historic town square, a sea-shell-shaped plaza called the Piazza del Campo. (Not all contradas are represented in each race. Each contrada is guaranteed one race each year, with some racing in both events.)

The horses are ridden bareback, and it's not uncommon for some jockeys to fall off their mount during the race. However, the winner of the Palio is the horse, not the jockey. So, if a riderless horse crosses the finish line first, that contrada is the winner. You can see the races on YouTube.

If you watch one of the Palio races (search "Palio Horse Race" on YouTube and you'll be entertained by the unique races), you'll be struck by what takes place after the winner crosses the finish line. A crowd—the members of the contrada—mobs the horse and jockey to extend congratulations. The winning contrada then moves through the streets to one of two cathedrals where they give thanks to God for their victory and subsequently hold a huge celebration.

Ask a member of a contrada what's one of the most important dates in their life and you'll likely get a story about the year their contrada won the Palio. It's that important.

Social scientists love to study Sienna and its unique neighborhoods, which act similarly to a family unit. They take great pride in their home. From a very young age, children learn the importance of the place they live. They often become flag bearers in the parades each contrada hosts in the days leading up to the Palio.

In the prologue, I mentioned that while this book mostly deals with small towns and rural America, the ideas can be applied to neighborhoods within larger cities, which is the case in Sienna. The larger unit is broken into neighborhoods that take pride in the place they live and work to help all within their borders. Their way of life has succeeded through the centuries in great part due to the high standards these communities have formed within the city. It can be an example for not only small towns but also neighborhoods in larger cities.

It could be argued the contradas take community building to the extreme, creating a barrier for anyone new to join the group. It's something towns must guard against. It's great to form a neighborly feeling;

however, that feeling can't come at the expense of those who are new and make them feel unwelcome or like an outsider.

That said, consider what each contrada does to inspire its community to be a vital part of the larger city:

- Everyone is made to feel like family. The neighborhood's colors, crest, and symbol are visible on the buildings and are often a part of the clothes one wears.
- There's a visible identification with the community in which they live. Most residents are baptized into their contrada from a fountain in the neighborhood. Obviously, your town doesn't have to go to this extreme, but people have a connection with the place they live.
- There are neighborhood and city events in which individuals participate as a contrada. These events involve the youth and show great pride for the place in which one lives.
- Because there is a sense of family, the neighborhood places high regard on the health and well-being of its citizens. The poor receive help, crime is low, the streets are clean, and the people of a neighborhood seek to create a vibrant community.
- There are special annual events that bring the community together and attract others to the neighborhood and the city. These events further accentuate the pride in the city and the welcoming atmosphere to guests. Sienna is consistently ranked as one of the favorite stops visitors make in Italy due to many of these factors.

So how do you create a friendly and welcoming place to live? Examples such as Nancy, Fred, and the residents of Sienna provide some insights. We can put some data behind the question as well. A few years ago, *Forbes* magazine worked with Nextdoor.com in attempt to define and rank "friendly" communities. Perhaps what was most interesting was some of the common factors friendly places share.

Home ownership provides stability in a neighborhood, which tends to create friendly places to live. Higher rates of charitable giving are another data point that can signify a welcoming place to live. Low crime and the percentage of college graduates are also important. There's a correlation between higher education and civic involvement and volunteerism.

The study also identified factors we discussed earlier in this chapter. Are there town events, festivals, and parades? Are there movies or concerts in the park? Friendly towns often have a higher percentage of green space compared with other cities. Those "friendlier" towns tend to have more parks, recreational trails, and other places for physical activity.

I was recently speaking in a community where a planning meeting was being held for an addition to a recreation area. A 20-something young man offered his opinion: "I want this not only because I will use it but also because other nearby towns don't have it and that could influence others to want to come live here."

What he was articulating is what the data confirm. People want to live in places where there are more opportunities to see, do, and experience life. Those experiences tend to bring people together in a welcoming atmosphere, thus creating friendlier places to live. It's the difference between someone living in a house and someone finding their home.

We've discussed several ways towns have been successful in building vibrant communities. Here are some takeaways I've observed from places doing this well:

- Vibrant communities know what makes them "special." It could be odd or quirky. It could be something that's been there for decades or something developed out of the blue. It's all right to have the double-decker outhouse or the largest ball of twine or to dub yourself "The Carousel City." It makes your place special.
- Vibrant communities are visually attractive communities. It could be flower baskets on the street lights, a well-kept downtown, or restored brick buildings.
- Vibrant communities have events, festivals, recreational activities, and attractions for all ages that help build a sense of community.
- Vibrant communities have a mix of special events and permanent opportunities. There's something for the visitor as well as the resident. If your community doesn't offer

vibrant opportunities throughout the year, people are likely to find them elsewhere, perhaps making a permanent move from the community.

Building a friendly atmosphere is important yet hard to define and attain. Communities must work to be welcoming, proactive, and forward-thinking, which can be done by a welcoming liaison or committee. Ultimately, that atmosphere is best achieved by building a feeling of community within the residents who take pride in where they live and welcome others to join them in building a vibrant place to call home.

CHAPTER 4

The Next Generation

I n the 1990s, Heartland Health, the hospital serving St. Joseph and surrounding counties in northwest Missouri and northeast Kansas, had a novel idea to establish a hospital foundation. Today, almost every hospital has a foundation that helps raise funds to purchase medical equipment and update facilities.

As mentioned in chapter one Heartland Hospital's CEO, Lowell Kruse, saw a challenge looming on the horizon. The people living in the counties the hospital serves were above the state and national averages for obesity and the number of smokers. In fact, those counties lagged in several critical areas of health.

The area was also failing to retain young people. The best and brightest were heading to large metro cities, which in turn was impacting the economic welfare of the region.

Lowell, and many others at Heartland Health, decided the success of the hospital rested on reaching far beyond the walls of the facility. They needed to impact lives not only in the present but also in the future. Heartland also broadened the definition of "health" beyond just the immediate decisions impacting one's body.

"The foundation of improving a community is educational attainment," Lowell said of the decisions made in the 1990s. "Let's focus on kids as much as we can. Let's focus on communities and what we can do to help bring communities together."

Heartland Foundation's shift in focus might be traced all the way back to 1993 when the hospital made the decision to join the National Healthy Communities Movement, led by the Healthcare Forum. Judy Sabbert started as a grants manager at Heartland and moved into leadership in 1989, serving as president of the foundation until her retirement in 2016.

"The Forum's thinking was that when diverse partners from various sectors like health care, business, education, social service, the faith community, and government come together, you can accomplish so much more for one's community than when working alone or within just one sector," Judy recalled.

"Health" was described very broadly. It certainly meant physical health and well-being, but it included economic factors, community and civic engagement, quality of life, and a host of other factors. "Research indicated that the two best or leading indicators of a healthy community relate to higher levels of education, such as college and job certification programs, and good-paying jobs," Judy emphasized. "When those two indicators are at high levels, the health of individuals, the health of a population, and the health of a community rise."

It was clear education was vital in creating a healthier community. If a health care organization wanted to improve the health of the region, it needed an educational partner. That's where Northwest Missouri State University entered the picture. Judy partnered with Bob Bush, vice president of the Center for Applied Research at the university, to first create a Community Transformation Forum. People of all ages (middle school to senior citizens) from diverse backgrounds were invited to engage in a three-day process to look at their communities.

While the forums proved beneficial to the communities, Judy said there was an unexpected outcome that would position the course of the foundation for decades to come. "One of the 'ahas' we discovered is that bringing young people to the table was critical," she recalled. "In fact, it changed the conversations, working in both small groups and the larger gathering."

Heartland Foundation and Northwest Missouri State University partnered with the University of Minnesota and its Center for Democracy and Public Discourse. The project called Public Achievement is a youth social justice movement tied to schools. "We began to realize the importance of the youth voice," Judy explained. "They saw things differently and were not jaded by an attitude of 'we could never do that' or 'it simply won't work.' They courageously and thoughtfully spoke their minds in hopes the adult community would listen and recognize their value. Many times, the youth would step forward to lead a group. It was an amazing dynamic that we observed."

The number of students whom they could involve in the Public Achievement project and the transformation forums was limited due to other school activities that competed for their time. There had to be a way to reach more students and create learning that was a part of the school day. "The best way to do so was to work closely with schools," Judy said.

She had seen her own children participate in experiential learning programs through the Learning Exchange in Kansas City. "I observed, as a parent volunteer, that the students were highly engaged in the learning process, even having fun. It was hands-on learning that appealed to all children with different learning styles," she said.

Judy's experience at the Learning Exchange led to the question: "Why couldn't Heartland Foundation do something similar, only focusing on a civics empowerment model?" They could build their own program, creating a hands-on experience that would empower youth to take the lead and see the promise of the rural and small towns in which they live.

When Heartland Health acquired this building, the roof was literally falling in on a portion of the structure. The site was transformed into emPowerU, an experiential learning center were middle-school students come to learn about the power they have to transform their community for the better. Grants are provided to put many of their ideas into practice.

The original and current "campus" of the emPowerU program is housed in a renovated warehouse space in downtown St. Joseph. The roof was literally falling in when Heartland Foundation acquired it. Reclaiming an old building in downtown also served to make a statement: the foundation's mission was to turn around communities, and it would begin with the very building in which it was housed.

The foundation worked with the Learning Exchange to create a curriculum to empower middle school–aged students to take the lead in their communities and realize the power they had to make positive change. Students would complete the curriculum in their local schools and, at the end of the program, take a field trip to emPowerU to apply what they had learned. It is an innovative, hands-on experience where youth problem-solve community issues.

The capstone project required the students to develop a presentation about a change they wanted to see in their community. They presented their ideas (complete with PowerPoint slides and supporting evidence) to a mock city council.

What those students didn't realize was the "mock" council was often real city council members from the region. That moment, when students presented their ideas to the adults, was powerful. Suddenly, a region's leaders are face-to-face with the youth, and those youth are talking about the changes they'd like to see in their hometown.

The foundation also awards grants to some of the projects the youth develop through emPowerU. It's a transformative experience for a middle school–aged group to identify, study, and present a solution to a local challenge and then receive the funds to implement their solution.

In 2016, a second "campus" opened in King City, Missouri (population 1,013), about a half hour northeast of St. Joseph. The idea is to bring the experience to more students in the area.

Kansas State University has been evaluating the program from the beginning. Marks have been high, and the work of empowering students to see opportunities has been great. Equally important has been the experience for adults to listen to the youth of their hometowns.

In an eight-year period, hundreds of pages of results have been collected. Perhaps the best evaluations have come from some of the students themselves. One wrote, "I think emPowerU is a good place because it helps students think about their future." Another wrote, "A strength I discovered about myself was being able to make a stand."

Many hospitals that focus on a hospital fund-raising mission have two or three people on their foundation staff. Heartland Foundation, however, chose a different path strengthening communities in the region. It has close to 10 full-time members, plus many part-time facilitators for emPowerU and other outreach programs.

As one chairman of the Heartland Foundation board told me, "Our ultimate mission is to put our parent company out of business!" In other words, if the foundation's programs succeeded, the education and work-place opportunities for youth in the region would increase, which, in turn, would boost the overall health of the region, decreasing the number of patients the hospital needed to see.

Of course, no program could achieve that level of success, and a certain number of people need a hospital for a myriad of reasons, but the point was powerful: Their mission was to transform the life of their small towns and rural America by changing the course of their youth for the better.

(During this period of time, the hospital changed names to Mosaic Life Care, but the foundation retained the name Heartland Foundation. Notice the word "hospital" does not appear in Mosaic's name, but rather "life care," indicating the mission to improve people's lives, not just treat them when they are sick.)

Heartland Foundation often referred to a "pyramid" developed by the National Civic League as a guide to what could be accomplished in communities. The pyramid was a powerful tool in painting a picture of why so much time, effort, and resources should be spent by the hospital to develop emPowerU and other innovative programs that work to improve the lives of the people and communities in their area.

About two-thirds of the hospital's patients were there due to lifestyle choices. For instance, heart disease might be the result of poor diet and lack of exercise over the course of many years. While the hospital will always have a mission to care for the sick, doesn't it make sense to try to influence healthy choices early in a person's life?

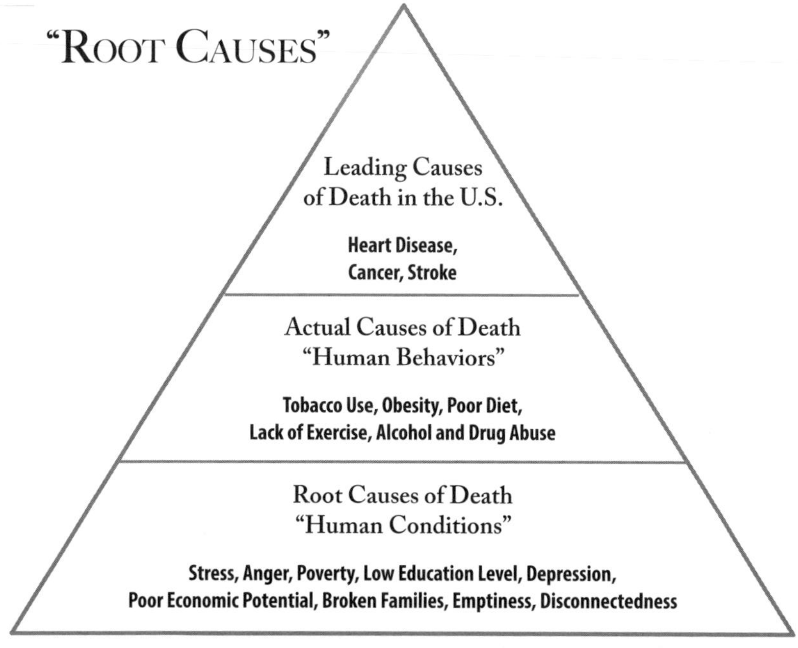

Adapted from National Civic League, Healthy Communities Conference. Updated with CDC Data and Best Practices.

The "Root Causes" pyramid helps demonstrate that the leading causes of death (heart disease, cancer, and strokes) are often the result of "human behaviors" and "human conditions." By working to "flip" the words at the base of the pyramid to their antonyms, communities can affect the long-term health and well-being of their region.

The top line of the pyramid shows the three leading causes of death in the United States are heart disease, cancer, and strokes. The mid-level of the pyramid shows human behaviors that often contribute to those killers, such as alcohol abuse, obesity, lack of exercise, and a poor diet.

At the base of the pyramid are the "root causes" or "human conditions" that might be precursors to those human behaviors. Here we find things such as stress, anger, poverty, poor education, depression, limited earning potential, broken families, and disconnectedness.

As Lowell Kruse told me, "If we didn't get to the root of that pyramid, we were going to keep fighting the same battles for decades to come."

Two points made in the pyramid stand out to me as vitally important to create the Total Town Makeover. First, research tells us the correlation between the levels of this pyramid is strong. The more items a person has on the bottom level of the pyramid, the more likely the items in the middle are true, which makes them more likely to have the actual causes of death at the top of the pyramid.

Second, communities have tremendous power to influence the overall well-being of people. If communities make it their mission to flip the characteristics at the bottom of the pyramid to their antonyms, then they will most likely create a healthier, better-educated, mentally stronger, longer-living, and wealthier place to live.

It can take years and decades to see the results. Consequently, many communities don't pursue change or give up too quickly. In a time when immediate results can be paramount, it's difficult to stick with something that takes a long time to pay off, even if it will produce positive results. But it's those long-term results that ultimately create the makeover.

"It gets a little foreign to what a hospital ought to be doing," Lowell said. "When you take the long view of what really drives health, it's educated, excited people working in communities around us and helping to improve everything in that community."

Most communities will readily acknowledge the importance of youth. However, those same communities often underestimate the power of the young people in their community and how to best engage them in building a better place to live in the future.

The late Peter Benson, CEO and president of the Search Institute, was a psychologist and pioneer in defining the "developmental assets" for youth. I had the honor of meeting and interviewing Dr. Benson on a couple of occasions. His books, such as *All Kids Are Our Kids,* and the work of the institute, are great reading for people of all ages.

The Search Institute is perhaps best known for defining "40 Developmental Assets" for different ages of students. These 40 assets have a direct correlation to the academic and personal success of kids. The more assets a student possesses, the more likely he or she is to excel in school and avoid activities that negatively impact his or her life.

As Dr. Benson told me, "There are not any 'gateway' assets." In other words, each asset is equal to the others in importance. You can't prioritize which asset a student should seek. However, some assets seem to be more elusive. In fact, one of the assets that consistently ranks near the bottom is "community values youth."

Interestingly, I often hear towns and schools tout how they value their youth. They are small enough to listen to their ideas, know their names, and personally care about their success. Yet, students consistently tell the Search Institute their community does not value them. Why do communities believe they do a great job supporting their youth, yet the youth don't say the same thing?

Many schools and communities know the names of their students. However, anyone beyond their classroom teacher and parents/guardians might be hard-pressed to tell you something specific about that student, such as she enjoys ice-skating or he has a puppy named George. There is a big difference between knowing someone's name and truly knowing them.

It might seem trivial to know the name of a kid's new puppy, but those minor details are important in developing the culture of educational success. One community in Texas believed it was so important to change its educational culture that it enlisted the help of school bus drivers—the first school staff to interact with students each day. They challenged their bus drivers to learn at least two new things about each student on their bus and engage the student in a quick conversation when they boarded. Did you go ice-skating this weekend? How is your puppy, George, doing?

Sounds simple—but few do it. Yet, doing so can have profound results. Students begin to realize their community values them and what is taking place in their lives. When students know others care about who they are and what they do, they begin their day on a more positive note.

In one high-performing school, I learned the staff and administration have a goal to greet students by name three times before they sit in their seat to begin the school day.

This means some teachers stand on the sidewalks where buses off-load students and where parents drop off their children. Administrators usually stand at the school doors to greet each student by name and engage in quick conversations. Homeroom teachers stand outside their classroom to greet each student before entering. It's no coincidence this school was one of the best in the state when ranked on a number of educational factors.

Any school that goes out of its way to engage students in that manner also works with students and families to create a positive learning environment. These types of schools are working to build the best culture at the bottom of that pyramid we discussed earlier. Remember, if you flip the words to their antonyms, you are affecting people's lives for the better for the long-term.

Perhaps you've noticed a common thread in this chapter about the importance of the next generation in creating a Total Town Makeover. This step involves adults and students working side-by-side in the process. Each truly values the contribution of the others. Remember Peter Benson and the Search Institute's research shows students often don't feel their community values their opinion. Communities working through the process of a successful makeover are finding ways to not only value the opinion of their youth but also put those ideas into action.

The Center for Mental Health in Schools and Student Learning Supports at UCLA works to bridge the gap between generations by finding ways to better connect one another. They note, "School staff must value volunteers and learn how to recruit, train, nurture, and use them effectively." Those schools that do this can enable "teachers to personalize instruction, free teachers and other school personnel to meet students' understanding and relations, enhance home involvement, and enrich the lives of volunteers."

It was perhaps best summarized by one of the center's volunteers who said, "When a community is very involved in their school volunteering, more people have a better sense of the total education picture and see how dedicated so many people are to educating the community's youth."

Henderson and Mapp in their work, *A New Wave of Evidence: The Impact of Schools, Family, and Community Connections on Student Achievement*, note the importance of volunteers in schools can be significant. They reported, "Volunteers are viewed as contributing to better school attendance, improved grades and test scores, matriculation, less misbehavior, better social skills, staying in school, graduating, and going on to college."

If the above list is not enough reason to get the community involved in schools, the authors also observed volunteers tended to show students they took education seriously and promoted better school climate.

It is my observation most schools welcome *the thought* of having volunteers. However, follow-through is more difficult. There are necessary hurdles to insure volunteers have background checks and a system in place to use their talents. In addition, with the pressure of the "essentials," volunteer programs are often not at the forefront of thought in schools.

It is also my observation that schools in small towns sometimes don't appreciate the importance of volunteers because they operate under the notion the community is small, everyone knows one another, and, therefore, it's not as important. Also, in small towns, work ethic is important. If teachers were to welcome volunteers, would they be seen as "lazy" because they "need help" in the classroom?

The above challenges can be addressed, and once a program is up and running, the barriers tend to vanish over time. Consider the following: What if I told you there was a no-cost way you could immediately begin to improve the school's atmosphere, positively affect the learning environment, provide more resources, improve test scores, and show students their community not only values education but also values them personally? Wouldn't you immediately want to implement that program? Sure!

OK, maybe there are some costs for background checks and organizing the volunteers, but they are minimal in comparison to the benefits. Some of the most successful *public* schools in the nation now *require* parents/guardians to volunteer a certain number of hours at their children's school. In cases where there is a choice of schools, these "mandatory volunteering" schools are often the highest achieving and most popular. When adults are involved in the school, good things happen. Communities that value youth and the characteristics at the base of that pyramid will produce positive, lifelong results.

Best-selling author Malcolm Gladwell, in his book *Outliers*, devoted research to determine the differences between high-achieving students and schools and low-achieving students and schools. One intriguing result was found when measuring the test scores and advancement of students from "low-, middle-, and high-income" families. Data showed the students from high-income families achieved better results and advanced at a quicker pace academically than those in middle- and low-income families.

However, when the data were organized to show *when* the educational gains took place, the research showed students from high-income families widened their gap during the summer. "Middle- and upper-middle-class families are using weekends and summer vacation to push their children ahead," Gladwell wrote. He noted many of these students, thanks to their parents, visit museums, enroll in special programs, and go to summer camp where they take classes. They generally have access to books at home and perhaps visit the library.

Consider this story Steven Mitchell shared with me about Calico Rock. The town opened a Science Center and Art Gallery in one of the buildings purchased by the local museum board. One summer afternoon an older car pulled up in front of the building. Three kids jumped out of the car, begging four adults, presumably parents and grandparents, to get out and come inside the building.

Part of the revitalization effort in Calico Rock, Arkansas, included a science center and art gallery. Those facilities provide opportunities for students, families, and schools to come to the site throughout the year. Portions of both the science center *(next page)* and the art gallery *(above)* are shown here. No admission is charged, but a gift shop and conference room (available for rental) offset operation costs. The building provides educational opportunities for students in the region year-round.

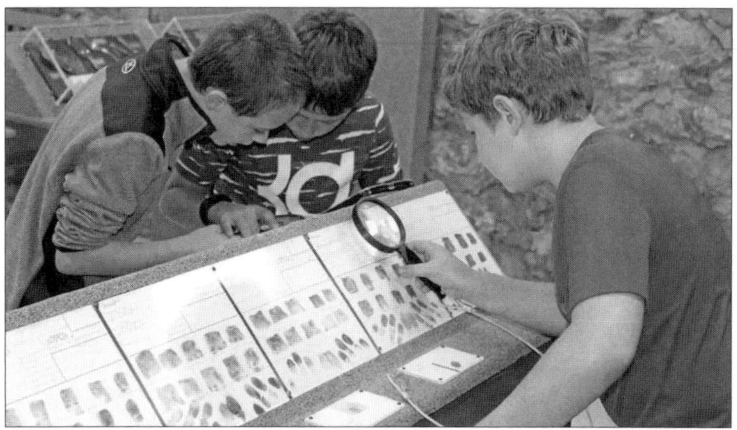

One kid exclaimed, "Hurry, I want you to see what we did when we came here with our school." Grandma and Grandpa slowly followed the young kids into the building. The kids ran around the place pointing out all they had seen and learned on their school trip.

Grandma seemed a bit lost in the whole experience. She wandered toward the volunteer on duty with a perplexed look on her face. "You may need to help me," she said to the volunteer.

"How can I help?" the gallery volunteer responded.

"Well, I'm 82 years old," Grandma said, "and this is the first time I've ever been in a museum. I'm not sure what I'm supposed to do."

Tears welled up in the volunteer's eyes. "Well, you can do anything you want," the volunteer said. "We're glad you're here!"

The volunteer learned the family had traveled 20 miles over crooked roads to get to Calico Rock. The kids went to school in another town and had visited the museum on a class field trip. They had so much fun, and the free admission was a draw for the family.

When giving presentations on revitalizing small towns, Mitchell points to Calico Rock's Science Center and Art Gallery as an important part of the educational process. "Those experiences help provide *all* kids with learning during the summer. We want to inspire kids to come back and keep learning. That opportunity wasn't available with an empty storefront, but it is now thanks to the work of volunteers who saw what we could do for our community and area."

Heartland Foundation offers summer camps at its facilities to further learning. The town of Shickley, Nebraska, has hosted summer entrepreneurship camps for kids. The key is making these opportunities available to all students and providing a fun and educational experience. These examples show how a *community* can help students learn year-round through various opportunities.

"Schools work," Gladwell pointed out. "The only problem with school, for the kids who aren't achieving, is that there isn't enough of it." The gaps occur in the three summer months. Schools might have innovative programs to help narrow that gap, but communities such as Calico Rock, St. Joseph, and Shickley are playing an important role by truly valuing their youth.

At this point, I haven't mentioned anything about the actual academic performance of a school. That doesn't mean it's not important—it's extremely important. Every school, regardless of size, needs to set a high bar and work to help students achieve it. Each school is most likely evaluated (for better or worse) on standardized test scores.

But schools in smaller communities have a unique benefit—and challenge—all wrapped into one. Their future success might lie in not only educating their students but also empowering them to see the difference they can make right at home. When students feel valued and empowered, their grades often improve as well.

This is why programs such as Heartland Foundation's emPowerU are so important. They change the focus of student empowerment, allowing all students to share their ideas and excel.

Communities are finding success by creating opportunities for students and adults to work side-by-side on projects that move schools and towns forward. Consider Purdy, Missouri. The town of just over 1,000 is located in the southwestern corner of Missouri. In 2006, when Gerry Wass became the foreign language instructor, he inherited a fledgling Spanish club as part of his duties.

"A couple of students asked me, 'Isn't there something we could do for community service?' Gerry said as we sat down to talk about a project that grew from that simple question. Some of his students needed community service hours to bolster applications for college.

Gerry told me the school and community were saturated with clubs selling items to raise money. He and the students were looking for something different that would be more beneficial for the area. He wondered about starting a recycling program. Neither the school nor town had one, and the project could not only count toward community service but also serve as a fundraiser for the foreign language club.

The students began collecting recyclables from the school and took them to a nearby recycling center. While they were happy to do something worthwhile, they were discouraged because they received none of the profits.

So, the club began to look for ways to store recycled materials and then work with a vendor to earn money. Their first real profit came from aluminum cans, but the cans took up too much space. A local paving roller came in handy.

"We spread all of the aluminum cans over the parking lot, then we ran over them with the paver, and then we shoveled them into bags," Gerry said. The school principal hauled the cans to Joplin, Missouri, and brought back the first cash for the club.

While smashing cans with a paving roller is an interesting sight to see, it was not the best route for long-term profit growth. "We had nothing to do with the most valuable thing we had, which was cardboard," Gerry realized. In fact, the school had an incinerator to get rid of it. Perhaps the club could recycle it? Their first grant from the local solid waste district supplied a cardboard baler.

Eventually, the club income grew to over $5,000 per year—hard work but a community service project that was keeping items out of landfills and turning it into money. The money was spent on activities for the club's students, which numbered as high as 75 in some years. "That eventually began to trouble me—that we were only spending the money on ourselves," Gerry said.

So, they began to look for ways to use their resources to help their small town. They started small, purchasing a couple of barbeque grills for the park near the school. One of the students commented, "Isn't there something we can do to improve this old playground next to the school?"

And that's when others in Purdy took notice. Adults formed a group to help the club's mission. "That led to the organization of an adult group to assist us with the project," Gerry explained. "The Purdy Recycling Project added a sister organization, the Purdy Renewal Project."

The group affiliated themselves with the Community Foundation of the Ozarks, and soon the two organizations were tackling even bigger projects. Gerry said his message to students was simple: "Do this because it makes you feel good about yourself, not because someone says that you should do community service."

Gerry has since retired from teaching, but the fundraising model that also served as a community service project is one that is still working well in Purdy. It was a project that in turn inspired adults in the community to work alongside their youth to create positive changes in their hometown.

Travel up Interstate 44 a couple of hours from Purdy and you'll come to the town of St. James, with a population of just over 4,000. In 2011, Terrill Story helped organize a Youth Empowerment Project (YEP) chapter. Terrill had been assisting the local high school as a counselor and was later hired to teach art, a position he still holds at the school. With the help of a grant, the YEP group renovated an old city firehouse and turned it into a coffee shop.

At the time, high school principal Keith McCarthy said, "I thought nothing short of a stick of dynamite would help the place [the old firehouse]." The city allowed the group to lease the building for $5 per month. They also brought the building into code compliance.

Firehouse Coffee Shop was born later that year. Students operate the business after school. During the day, a variety of volunteers help. For young people, it's a great way to gain on-the-job experience, especially for those who might have an interest in the culinary field. Art students helped brighten the interior. They also found old fire gear and pictures of the building when it was in use as a firehouse and used those items as interior decor. It was a melding of the old and new, and a merging of youth and adults, to create a needed business. "This should be a place of continuity, a place to pay it forward and invest in something," Terrill said.

Terrill Story (back row, middle), along with other student and adult volunteers in the community of St. James, Missouri, helped turn the old firehouse into a coffeehouse. Students volunteer to work the business after school, and the proceeds are used to cover expenses and fund charitable causes voted on by the students themselves. The space has become a spot where students, faculty, and community members can gather to work, visit, and relax.

Such projects take time and planning. In some cases, they take money, but communities are usually supportive of such efforts. Most importantly, they address the "community values youth" asset often lacking when the Search Institute evaluates the young people of a specific place. Efforts such as those in St. James not only empower students but also teach skills and can provide an economic impact.

In Shickley, Nebraska, the community supports a regular "entrepreneurship camp" where students are taught a summer curriculum by local teachers based on work from the University of Nebraska Extension. The students develop their own business ideas and receive starter funds to produce products they then sell at a community event during the summer. The camp helps students understand how to build a business, and it helps the community see their kids as young people who have great ideas about developing new products.

How do you inspire students to further their education, build skills, and improve their community at the same time? El Dorado, Arkansas, is a good place to look. The town of under 20,000 lagged behind similar towns in education as they entered the twenty-first century. High school enrollment had decreased by 10% in the 15 years prior to 2005. It was then a local company, Murphy Oil, decided to begin a program to bolster education and the community.

In 2006, they committed $50 million to a program today called the El Dorado Promise. It is modeled after a program first begun in Kalamazoo, Michigan. Students in El Dorado do not have to meet financial aid or grade point requirements to receive a scholarship. The program pays up to the highest in-state public university rate for tuition and mandatory fees for any student enrolled since ninth grade in El Dorado. Students who attend school there all 12 grades can receive 100% of their college fees paid. The scale slides to 65% for those enrolled since ninth grade.

Imagine the impact on a town and school system if any student who wanted to attend college could do so—and have their tuition paid? In 2016, 84% of the students in high school eligible for the program attended college. That compares to the state average of 50%.

El Dorado's population and school enrollment were on a steady decline. Now, they are trending upward. In fact, El Dorado's enrollment rose over 15% compared with what was projected without such a scholarship program in place.

Test scores and student involvement have increased as well. With 84% of students attending college, there's an important reason to prepare for the education they'll receive after high school graduation. The number of AP classes offered have increased. Students can receive the scholarship for five consecutive years as long as they maintain a 2.0 grade point average and take at least 12 credit hours per semester.

The community has grown in more than just number of students. This is a place people want to live and work. There's a feeling of pride—a feeling this small town can do things other towns cannot. This wasn't the case a decade or more ago.

You might say, "I wish someone would hand us $50 million to start such a program." Certainly, the donation by Murphy Oil was a huge catalyst to make all of this happen. But is such a goal out of reach for others? Could your town design a program to pay half of the cost? Perhaps you could fund the first two years? Could you find businesses and individuals committed to providing the seed money for an endowment to accomplish this? These first steps are possible, and they can make a large difference, beyond sending more students to college.

Nearby Arkadelphia, Arkansas, began a Promise program, as well. Their town is smaller than El Dorado, at a population of just over 10,000. The program is tailored to meet the needs of their students and was part of the county's master planning efforts. In Arkadelphia, the Promise scholarships can pay up to $4,000 for the freshman year of college. Amounts can vary for subsequent years depending on other scholarships and grants the student has earned.

The program in Arkadelphia is not as old as the one in El Dorado, but the statistics are already promising. In the first year the Promise scholarships were offered, 74% of graduating seniors attended college, compared with about 60% in years prior.

Perhaps the most striking accomplishment, though, is the retention rate of Arkadelphia students who stay in college from their freshman year to their sophomore year. The retention rate was about 82%, over 20% higher than the state average and over 15% higher than the national average.

I have presented many programs to teachers over the years, many of which have been for smaller school districts. I often ask, "How many of you graduated from this high school?" It's not uncommon for a third of the hands to shoot up in the air. I then ask, "How many of you graduated from a school within 30 minutes of here? Another half of the audience will raise their hands.

The reality is for many schools in small-town America, the staff is largely from that school or close by. I then ask, "Why do you live here?" Some might say because their spouse lived in the area, but most acknowledge they are teaching in the school because it is "home" and they like the area. I will then follow up and ask, "How many of you have shared with your students why you made this your home?"

The truth is many educators and residents of small towns never share with young people why they chose to live there. Consider this story of the power of simply sharing why you live where you do. I interviewed a young man named Brad from a small Midwestern town. He was a high-achieving student from a small high school that graduated about 40 students each year.

His grades afforded him an opportunity to go to an Ivy League school, and he secured the scholarships to attend Harvard. The school and community were proud of Brad. A student from their small school was headed to, arguably, the top college in the nation. It was literally front-page news in the local paper.

Fast-forward two decades, and where is Brad now? The same hometown from which he graduated.

Stop and think about the sentence you just read. Brad is back in the small town where he grew up. What happened to Brad?

For most of us, our mind immediately moved to a scenario in which Brad dropped out of college. Maybe he didn't have the grades he needed to succeed at Harvard. Maybe the small-town school from which he graduated couldn't prepare a student for such a prestigious institution.

Actually, quite the opposite was true. Brad graduated with honors and worked for a time for a large multinational company. But after several years in some of the nation's and world's largest cities, he returned to his local community to be the CEO of the largest business in town.

His family didn't own a business or land for him to take over. He could earn a larger income somewhere else. His town was over 90 minutes from a large city with the amenities he had experienced elsewhere.

If you ask Brad why he lives in his small hometown, he talks about three individuals who influenced his decision. His grandfather shared with him why he liked the small town and the opportunities he saw there. In addition, a local insurance agent and the CEO of the community hospital told him on multiple occasions, "Brad, if you come back, we will find a job for you."

Most small towns and school districts would celebrate one of their graduates who was heading to Harvard. It is certainly something to be celebrated. Now imagine a small town that sent one of their own to Harvard and they got him back! They got him back!!

It is a message for every school and small town. You must shout the message loud and clear: "We want you back!" But you have to back it up with giving them a reason to come back. It begins by telling the story of why you made it your home and then committing yourself to making it the best and most welcoming place it can be. Brad came back because people in his community shared the story of why they liked the community and how he could be a part of the town's future.

I was recently visiting with the commissioner of education for a Midwestern state. He grew up in a small town and went on to teach at several schools, become an administrator, and earn a doctoral degree, and, eventually, he was named the Secretary of Education for the state. This gentleman had a great attitude and outlook on life. Although he was no longer living in small-town America, but rather the state's capital, he still looked at the needs of those in rural areas.

He reflected on a recent visit back to the town where he grew up and got his first teaching job. His words to the school and community were not meant to be harsh, but rather motivation to share a different story with the town's students. He said, "I told the people in my hometown audience, 'You told me success was leaving, so I did.'"

Whether it's said aloud or not, it's a feeling many students have in small-town America. If you truly want to be a success and if you want others to see you've made something of yourself, you need to leave.

In their book, *Hollowing out the Middle: The Rural Brain Drain and What It Means for America*, Patrick Carr and Maria Kefalas examine several factors affecting small towns and rural America. The couple even moved to a small town in Iowa so they could get a first-hand experience in the heartland.

They interviewed several graduates of the local high school and made the following observation on how that town and many other small towns view their youth. "Preparing the most talented young people to leave and succeed has traditionally been the modus operandi of small towns, and a vital part of the town's civic pride is from the collective satisfaction of knowing the young person you watched mature, and whom you might have coached or taught to play an instrument, has succeeded elsewhere."

There's nothing wrong with providing great education to students looking to further their education. That should be the norm. Having kids such as Brad go from a small-town high school to Harvard is something to celebrate. However, small towns must challenge the mind-set they have little to offer a kid such as Brad. As noted in the chapters on the economy and vibrant communities, they might well have more to offer yet are shy to tout those qualities.

But the authors, Carr and Kefalas, share another factor important to building the future for the next generation in small-town America. "A critical component of this effort is a more equitable distribution of resources to help Stayers build skills so they can compete in a postindustrial economy," they write.

The conclusion is more collaboration between schools and local colleges. "Rural schools should work to target programs in which non-college bound high school students can take courses for dual credit at a community college. This would help them acquire skills that would be fungible in the modern economy and not just be used toward a four-year degree."

If communities are forward-thinking and identify the workforce they *will* need, they can better position their students to take advantage of local jobs. The small town gets a better-educated, higher-earning, well-trained workforce to accomplish the multitude of jobs in rural America that do require further education after high school.

Perhaps their work is best summed up by this view of how small towns must begin to work with the next generation. "Given that young people are now rural America's most precious declining resource, it seems the best way to preserve the nation's small towns will be to create new sorts of conservation efforts to invest more efficiently in these young people, whose futures—as parents, workers, homeowners, voters, and taxpayers—will be so critical to the countryside's survival."

A few years ago, I learned of a powerful example of how communities and schools should be thinking about their futures. The folks in Brookfield and Marceline, Missouri, had a unique gift they gave their graduating seniors each year. They gave each graduate a mailbox.

Each mailbox has the student's name on the side, plus a logo of the school and town. Inside the mailbox is a DVD. On the DVD are pictures and a video of previous graduates of the school who have decided to make their home there. They've built businesses and grew families in that community. The DVD told their story.

Brookfield and Marceline, Missouri, annually give their graduating high school seniors personalized mailboxes. They hope graduates will consider putting their mailboxes in their hometown someday. The mailboxes also serve as a reminder to the community to "create a place where a student wants to put their mailbox."

The speech from the high school principal at the end of every graduation sounds something like this:

Before we conclude our graduation ceremony today, we have a gift from our community to each of the graduates.

Each of you is entering a portion of your life where you'll begin a career, perhaps you'll marry and have a family, AND you'll make a home. Wherever you make your home, you'll have a place you go to get your mail. You'll have a mailbox.

Each of the graduates today is receiving a personalized mailbox. Why a mailbox?

We want you to think about where you'll put your mailbox someday. Your mailbox signifies the place you call home. We hope you'll consider making your hometown your permanent home, either now or in the future.

Inside the mailbox you'll find a DVD. It's full of pictures of graduates from our high school, just like you, who decided to make this the place they live and work. We have invested time in your education. We want you back!

At this point the principal turns her attention to the crowd and delivers what should be the mantra for every town in the nation:

The mailboxes are also a reminder to all of us who live here. We've placed our mailbox in this school district. Let's do our best to create a community where students want to put their mailbox!

Think about it. Have you and I done everything we can to create a place were a kid wants to put their mailbox? It's about not just your hometown but every hometown in the nation.

Sometimes kids don't know how much you really value them until you just tell them so. There's one important caveat. While it's great for family members to encourage young people to consider building careers and families in rural America, it's vital for them to hear that message from others in the community.

If you encourage a young person who isn't in your family to consider making it their home someday, a couple of important things might just happen. First, the encouragement takes on more value because it comes from someone outside the child's family who might receive no direct benefit from their decision to reside in the area. Second, encouraging young people to consider your hometown makes you more likely to do things to make the community more appealing for them.

While the mailbox message is a vital one, it's also a message that can't wait to be told until high school graduation. It's a message that should be lived throughout life for it to truly have an effect on the students and adults who live in a community.

Don't get the wrong idea. I'm not saying students shouldn't be encouraged to check out other communities, travel to faraway places, and get work experiences they can't find locally. Those are great things to do, and they should be encouraged. Several will choose to make a home somewhere else. They should also be celebrated and encouraged. Hopefully, they feel their hometown helped provide the skills they needed to succeed wherever they put down roots. If so, they will perhaps stay connected to where they grew up. Maybe that hometown will be the place they retire. At the very least, it might be a place they support through gifts to a local endowment or scholarship fund.

Also, don't feel you've failed if a child in your family chooses to live somewhere else, even far from home. After one of my speeches, I visited with the parents of a couple of adult children who had settled elsewhere. They felt bad their kids didn't come back to the place they grew up. That's not the point. Help kids succeed wherever they might see their future. The point is work to build a place where a next generation would want to call home and you'll probably find a next generation that's more likely to make it their home. Whether they do so or not, you've helped them succeed.

Don't feel shy to tout the benefits of a home and career in small-town America. If you desire a total town makeover, the success of that dream will ultimately rest in those coming after you. You need those young people, whether they grew up there or not. Remember the words of the high school principal who simply said, "Let's make this a place where a kid wants to put their mailbox."

On the farm, my father would sometimes say to me, "I'm not doing this for me; I'm doing it for you." He meant he would not see the ultimate success of the work he was doing at that time. He was simply laying the foundation so I might more fully experience the fruits of that work someday. Such is the case for a portion of what you will do in your total town makeover. We are creating a makeover not only for our lifetime but also for the generations who follow.

Chapter 5

Make It Happen

My kids once attended an "invention camp." One of the first assignments they were given was to build a boat from tape, cardboard, drinking straws, and other items. The boat not only had to float but also had to be able to carry the weight of 25 pennies.

Some of the kids in the group asked for directions to build the boat. The teacher explained there were not any directions; this is how inventors work—they take the tools they have and begin designing a device that will accomplish the goal. It might take some trial and error to get the device to work, and there might be more than one way to accomplish the goal.

The total town makeover is much the same. There was a time when I was searching for the perfect handful of towns to highlight in this chapter to use as examples of what a successful total town makeover would look like. I eventually came to the conclusion an effective makeover will look different for almost every town in America.

However, the tools to create a makeover are often similar. That's why I've broken those tools into the areas of the economy, vibrant communities, and next-generation focus. Like fashioning a boat to hold those pennies, there is no one way to accomplish the goal. The idea has to float in your hometown. Some ideas float better than others depending on where you live. We have to examine the tools at hand and figure out the best way to begin.

That said, the path forward starts with the people in the community. How do you encourage others to join in and build a team to make it happen?

I once attended a meeting where a friend of mine was speaking to a group of townspeople about changes they wanted to see in their community. A local group of concerned citizens had organized the meeting to begin the makeover process and my friend was providing input to their gathering.

I sat in on the meeting for about a half hour and would say it was going "just all right." That's Midwestern jargon for everyone was polite and listened, but it wasn't the type of meeting that inspired you to go out and make a difference in your town.

At the end of the meeting, I figured my friend would have something positive to say since he was the expert brought in to provide ideas. He looked at me and quietly said, "They don't have the right people on the bus."

I asked him what he meant, and he said, "Did you see the body language of the people in the audience? They are receptive to the message, but they don't have the right messengers."

He politely gathered the small group of leaders and then shared some ideas of others who could join them in the effort. If they had additional leaders who better represented the entire town, their effort would be seen as a community-led initiative. Please understand he wasn't saying the original group couldn't accomplish the goal or didn't have the right vision. He was simply noting they didn't yet have all the people "on board" who would propel the vision forward.

I have made the case that one individual can do much to change and inspire a community. There are several examples of such people in this book. However, for changes to take place quicker and more thoroughly, it takes a group of committed citizens. There are some key factors to keep in mind when building that group.

I recently visited with a young lady who has spent several years working with and serving on local, regional, and state boards, many of which were volunteer efforts. She encourages each group to develop a list of skills and attributes that will help lead change.

Some of those areas of expertise might be found in people who work for:

- a municipal and/or county government
- a local nonprofit and/or civic group

- a school as a teacher or administrator
- a legal and/or accounting firm
- the media, communication, and promotion industry
- themselves as a businessowner

It's important to note you don't necessarily have to find a person who will fit each one of those categories. However, a framework for board membership will help you identify volunteers with a variety of skills and areas of knowledge to better tackle challenges.

Set parameters for term limits. Groups can stagnate and struggle when the same people have what can become a life term. If you don't want to lose the expertise of the veterans on the board, perhaps have them rotate off for a year and then be elected to serve again.

Above all, the people involved should be trustworthy and of good character. Benjamin Franklin said, "He that lieth down with dogs riseth up with fleas." The community won't trust the untrustworthy. Look for people whom others respect and who share the same vision.

So, what group should take the lead in a total town makeover? It could be a group already in existence. For instance, in Calico Rock, Arkansas, the local museum board took the lead. Sometimes it's difficult, though, for existing groups to shift their attention to revitalizing the town, because they must focus on initial goals specific to their group. For instance, the museum board's first goal was to build a museum. After accomplishing that goal, they progressed to purchasing buildings and growing businesses beyond what a museum board might be expected to accomplish.

You might want to consider rallying existing groups in town to form a "coordinating" effort comprised of members from the respective boards. This can be a good way to get representation and buy-in from existing organizations yet create a group united to help the entire community.

The coordinating group might consider a "town hall" meeting where local leaders can prioritize needs and goals. Compiling a list of three or four goals is a great way to begin.

Sometimes you don't get a lot of say in who is "on your bus." If you're a part of an elected or appointed board or governmental entity, your bus might have people with very different views. That shouldn't be an excuse for lack of progress, though. Encourage other progressively minded members of your community to run for local offices. They might have the ideas but lack the encouragement to run.

It's also key to take into account the ages of those in your group. Do you have representation from young adults (even someone from high school), families, retirees, etc.?

Experience is vital. However, if a group gets "too old," you lose a couple of important benefits. First, you potentially lose your appeal to the younger generation, which tends to draw inspiration from others in their peer group who are active in local groups.

Second, the younger folks have a different skill set than many of the older people in the group. For instance, I was recently working with a nine-member board, and the "middle-aged" person in the group was 45 years old. The oldest person was a 70-year-old retiree. The youngest person was in their late 20s.

When it came time to raise funds, the young people on the board felt a little uncomfortable reaching out to people a generation (or two) older than them. However, those in the older half of the group were more willing to reach out because they had longevity in the community and the people they were asking tended to be in their same age range.

However, when it came time to develop a website and video for the group, the younger board members were ready for the task, while the older members, though supportive, had a perplexed look on their faces. The younger members' skill set was perfect for the task, whereas most of the older board members had not mastered the skills of creating videos, building a website, and networking via social media.

One common challenge I hear is that it's hard to involve younger people who want to help. This can certainly be the case, but here are some ideas to get you over that hurdle.

Look for younger people in your community who possess a specific skill set that would benefit your board. Talk to them about how they can help. For instance, shooting and editing a video would take me a lot of time to learn, not to mention a lot of time to perform. For someone with experience, they might be able to perform the necessary task in their spare time and do so relatively quickly.

Reassure younger folks that your group will work with their schedule, which might include a busy family. Perhaps you can allow them to "attend" meetings via phone. Your group might not need to meet the second Tuesday of every month at 7:00. Could you have fewer in-person meetings but do more by connecting via email, phone calls, or the web?

My dad once gave me some valuable advice that he learned early on when hiring someone to work on the farm. "Set them up to succeed," he said. Give them a job they already know something about. Praise them. When they taste success in the small things, they will be ready to move on to bigger things. The same can be said for developing the members of your board.

That goes for cultivating publicly elected boards in your community as well. Encourage great young folks to run for city council, school board, and other groups. Serving others is a noble and worthwhile cause, but it can drain a person. Offer your encouragement and help. Notice the efforts they make.

Never underestimate the importance of a kind word or note. There have been times when I felt like I was part of a lost cause. There are times when you believe you're on a deserted island. In those times, all it takes is someone who offers a kind word, sends a nice text, or even writes a note of encouragement to make you feel like the journey isn't quite so daunting.

Someone once told me, "The sign of a great community is a place where people step forward and shake your hand not because they know you but rather because they don't." Great communities build a culture of welcoming the stranger and long-time resident alike. Changing that culture can be difficult, but it can begin with one person.

It's something I've tried to always remember. Encourage others. Praise them. Thank them. Do that for everyone, not just the folks you know. Remember Fred Mares (from our Vibrant Communities chapter) who worked at the Maryville, Missouri, Hy-Vee Supermarket? He was inducted into the company's Hall of Fame, mostly for his encouragement to others. Imagine that. A small-town hero whose superpower is encouraging others and making them feel good about themselves. He's never met a stranger. Every community needs someone like that!

But what about the difficult people?

Even if you get the right people on the bus, not everyone is going to like your bus. There will be some who see no need for your work or who think it's misguided or off track.

Rosabeth Kanter, author and professor at Harvard Business School, once said, "Change is disturbing when it is done to us, exhilarating when it is done by us." We might be excited about the changes we hope to make in our community. However, for others, it might feel like the change is happening to them. Change is disturbing. The goal is to get everyone on the exhilarating side of change.

My grandfather loved his time working with the Rural Electric Association. He was very passionate about bringing electricity to rural America. However, he told stories of people who not only didn't want electricity but also did all they could to make it difficult for others to get it.

He would often have to get permission to put in electric poles across a neighbor's property in order for someone farther down the road to get electricity. On occasion, the neighbors wouldn't grant permission. My grandfather would have to come up with alternate routes that cost time and money. It was easy to hold a grudge against those people. Many times, after a couple of years, those neighbors would realize they needed electricity and then want someone to come as fast as possible to put in poles. Such situations frustrated my grandfather.

Ron Drake, author of *Flip This Town*, the man I introduced earlier in the book who helped revitalize downtown Siloam Springs, talked of the challenges when it comes to organizing groups. After joining the Main Street organization in his hometown, he wrote: "When I joined the organization, half the board left, but the people who encouraged me to get involved in Main Street were excited. We wanted to make changes, and often times, that's difficult from some people."

In decades past, the organization had made progress but had begun to stagnate. "We wanted to do so much more for the long-term growth of the downtown core," Ron said. The goal, of course, is not for half of a group to quit, but it does show that groups sometimes go through a metamorphosis when tackling a new vision.

I once did an interview about a small town that had been struggling for a couple of decades. The townspeople saw the community was slipping away, but there seemed to be little energy among the existing groups to do much about it. I won't mention the town's name, as I'm sure those existing groups weren't actively trying to stymie their town's future, but they just didn't see the urgency.

Interestingly, the local Chamber of Commerce, the logical group to take the lead, couldn't agree on what to do. Worse yet, the group had leaders who simply didn't see the reason to revitalize the dying town. Some in the community had tried to work with the chamber to create change, but little happened.

In this case, a handful of visionary citizens formed their own group entirely focused on building new businesses in the community. Their goal was not to compete with the Chamber of Commerce but instead to focus on business development.

The effort worked. The new group had the right folks "on the bus." They were focused on a specific idea and had people who could help implement those ideas. I have heard the Chamber of Commerce still exists and does about as much as it's always done. Meanwhile, the other group continues to be the driver in making change happen. For the most part, the two groups get along, and there are some people who are members of both groups.

People and communities might suffer from the Baader-Meinhof phenomenon, or what is sometimes called the "frequency illusion." We've all experienced it. My wife and I wanted to purchase a SUV because our kids were growing and we needed more space to haul items to school and sports. We both particularly liked one model. We didn't think many people drove that SUV, but suddenly we kept noticing the particular model and pointing it out to one another. It seemed everyone had one.

The phenomenon occurs when we notice a specific thing or idea and then our subconscious mind begins looking for and noticing it. Remember when I mentioned Ron Drake said the biggest problem facing small towns is believing they can accomplish the goal? He calls it "restoration of the mind."

If your town only sees the negative and board members only remember everything that went wrong, the frequency illusion will continue to show more examples of why something will not work. It's a psychological barrier that must be overcome. It's my hope the examples in this book provide the real-life stories that show these changes are possible.

Another tip to overcome this challenge is to begin small, build momentum, and keep going. If people hear of a group trying to make changes yet never see any progress, they will quickly doubt there will be any progress. Accomplish the little things and then move on to the bigger things.

Makeover Checklist

There's no right or wrong way to accomplish the total town makeover, but I've found there are some common steps successful towns often take. Consider the following ideas to get started and keep the ball rolling:

- Does your town have an endowment and/or other sources of funding that can provide seed money for projects or matching funds for grants? Just as a person needs a savings account, endowments serve much the same purpose for a community.
- Do you have one group leading the way, or are separate groups pulling in different directions? Try to form a "coordinating group" or clearly define what each individual group hopes to accomplish.
- Does the community have short- and long-term goals? Have those goals been written down and presented to the public? People want to have an idea of the vision and goals before they buy in.
- Are you using the newspaper and social media to communicate? Provide progress updates. Show pictures. Build momentum. Social media allows you to connect with people who might not live nearby but have a connection to the town and will support your efforts too.

- Improve the town's culture by making a commitment to smile more and compliment and praise others. It might be a specific person or a group that lead the way in building a positive and proactive culture.

It was Rosebeth Kanter who said, "A vision is not just a picture of what could be; it is an appeal to our better selves, a call to become something more." She also said, "Leaders must pick causes they won't abandon easily, remain committed despite setbacks, and communicate their big ideas over and over again in every encounter."

In order to make change happen, we must have a vision that compels us to better ourselves and our community. There will be setbacks, but if you communicate the vision in each encounter, you will see positive changes.

Chapter 6

Why Not?

Many years have passed since that day my grandfather Maurice visited the little river town that didn't see the merit in electricity. In 1998, at the age of 95, he went to live in the local nursing home. As the months passed, it became more difficult for him to carry on a conversation, so I'd find myself talking about local and family events and he would simply listen.

One day, just as I was about to leave, I said, "Grandad, I'm going to speak to a group tonight. I thought I'd tell them the story about you trying to sell electricity."

He smiled, and suddenly you could tell that story from decades before perked his interest. He replied, "Did I ever tell you how that ended?"

"Yes, you told me. No one would buy electricity," I said.

Or, so I thought that's how it ended.

Perhaps sensing a bit of urgency, he mustered the strength to launch into the story and tell me more. He desired to tell another chapter—but also something important.

"I never went back there, at least to sell electricity," he said. "I was so mad I didn't really ever want to go back, but sometimes I had to drive over that way.

"One night I was driving along the river," he recalled. "It was winter, and all the leaves were off the trees. As I drove, I kept seeing something odd through the trees. It was like it didn't belong there, but I couldn't tell what it was. It looked like it was on the other bank of the river."

At this point in the story he paused, but only for an instant. His eyes seemed to stare into space. He was reliving the moment from 70 years prior. He was back on that dark river road.

"So, I pulled over, got out of the car, and walked over on the edge of the bluff," he said. "You know that bluff on the river, don't you?"

He looked at me for just an instant. I acknowledged I knew the bluff, and then his eyes went back to where they had been.

"I looked through the trees and across the river to that town that wouldn't buy electricity. Then I figured out what I was seeing. I counted 13 electric lights," he recalled.

It was quite apparent not only that he knew the exact number of lights but also, now, 70 years later, that he could still count them in his mind as he looked at that little town in the night sky.

"They had electricity. I don't know who went there and when they got it, but they got electricity," he said. But his words weren't necessarily ones of joy. There was still a tinge of anger that he was the one who had been chided about the merits of the power he could bring them.

"I knew no one could hear me, but that didn't stop me," he said. "I shouted across the river as loud as I could, 'Now you believe me, don't you!'"

And with that my grandfather turned to me, maybe much the way Mr. Loest had looked up at him from that park bench 70 years prior, and said, "I guess he was right, wasn't he? It just took them a little time to believe, didn't it?"

That was the last story my grandfather ever shared with me. He died a few days later.

Those words have been etched in my memory ever since. When I'm angry and frustrated—when I feel like no one cares and no one believes—I'm reminded, "Sometimes it just takes a little time for people to believe."

While that's an important point for us to keep in mind, it also comes with a caveat. It's not a mantra that means we should always hold to our views until people come around to our way of thinking. Always do what is right and don't abandon the vision, but realize slight adjustments sometimes need to be made to arrive at the goal.

While writing this book, the question "Why?" popped into my mind from time to time. Why bother? Why is it so important? Why should I care about a makeover?

Maurice McCrea raised purebred Angus cattle and showed them at locations across the nation, including the Kansas City Stockyards. He was also active in helping bring electricity to rural locations in northwest Missouri. One of the pieces of advice he gave his grandson (the author of this book) was to always keep sharing your vision to improve the world around you, because "sometimes it just takes a little time for people to believe."

The nearest "town" to my home is Berlin (like the city in Germany, but after World War I the locals began to pronounce it "Ber-lun"). When my dad was a kid, Berlin had a general store, gas station, blacksmith shop, poultry house, switchboard operator, and several homes. Today, fewer than 10 people live there. There is a church, but no businesses.

The next closest town is Fairport. When I was a kid, Fairport had a K–8 school, grocery store, gas station, bank, post office, café, and feed store. Today, Fairport might have 50 residents and a café. A mechanic's shop occupies the old school building where my mom once taught sixth through eighth grade in one classroom.

Beyond Fairport is King City and Maysville, both towns of around 1,000 people. Will my children write a chapter of this book and note these places lost schools, banks, post offices, and other businesses? Or, will they write about new stores and a generation that was inspired to make small-town America their home?

Why did Berlin and Fairport fade over the decades? Was it simply destiny? Was it because not as many people needed to live in rural areas to work the land and, as a result, the smallest of towns vanished? Is that the destiny for the towns we've focused on in this book? Are townspeople fighting a futile battle to save places destined to close?

I wrote the above paragraphs and began to doubt myself. Perhaps I was wrong. Maybe all of the investment and revival are a lost cause—and a total town makeover is short-lived.

Then I heard some good news. A former graduate of King City High School, Susan, bought one of the storefronts in town that had been closed for over two years. She's opening a restaurant.

I sent her a message, thanking her for supporting her old hometown. I also asked her, why bother with a small town in Missouri? After all, she was now a successful businesswoman living in New York City.

I thought she'd reply with a sentence or two. She ended up writing several paragraphs. Susan recounted how her brother had cancer when they we young and many local citizens pitched in to help her family while her parents tended to her brother and took him on extended trips to the hospital for treatment. Friends and neighbors hosted a birthday party for her and helped her get ready for picture day at the school when her parents were gone. She had many fond memories.

She wrote: "I loved growing up in King City and enjoy going back multiple times a year. I have been saddened by seeing many of the businesses close when someone retires. I grew up with my mom being a merchant as well as my aunt and have many fond memories of our community supporting the students of the school and the community as a whole. When the opportunity presented itself for my husband and I to purchase a restaurant that had been closed for a couple years I thought, 'Why not me?'"

It suddenly hit me. The question to ask is not "Why?" It's "Why not?" It also struck me I did a disservice to the communities in this book when I listed their population. The population of those towns is far larger than those living within the city limits. The population includes residents of places such as New York City who still have a connection to the place they called home. They want to see that hometown succeed. There are many people who are willing to say, "Why not me!"

There's a small town I've visited in northeast Nebraska called Wynot. The story goes when the town was to be platted, some neighbors approached the farmer who owned the land and asked if they could purchase a portion of the property to begin a town and lure a railroad to the area. His response: "Why not!" And the town of Wynot, Nebraska, was born.

Wynot, Nebraska, was named for a property owner who, when asked to give land to establish the town, said, "Why not?"

I've come to the conclusion for a total town makeover, small towns need to rename themselves "Wynot." Why couldn't we do this? What if we tried this? How can we make it happen? A positive approach will drive lasting change.

There's much more than hope residing in rural America. There are qualities in these areas that can't be experienced anywhere else. Qualities people still yearn for. Qualities that lead them to put down roots, nurture families, begin businesses, and build strong schools. Qualities worth preserving not for the sake of nostalgia but for the sake of a better future for all.

Susan concluded her note to me by saying: "I've owned a business in NYC for over 13 years, and I have learned that sometimes you have to be willing to think outside the box. I know many are quick with an idea or, at times, a criticism, but many aren't willing to invest the money or the time to see something happen. I'm hopeful this will spur others to take the plunge and also think, 'Why not me?'"

It's time to quit asking "Why?" and begin asking "Why not?" Yes, life in small-town America can sometimes be difficult. There are real challenges. However, there are also many opportunities. It takes individuals who are willing to step forward, look at what can be done, and see it through. It begins by simply saying, "Why not me!"

Bibliography

America's Friendliest Towns. Nexdoor.com and *Forbes*, https://nextdoor.com/friendliesttowns, 2018.

Benson, Peter L. *All Kids Are Our Kids.* San Francisco: Jossey-Bass, 2006.

Binerer, Ahmet, Michael, Butler, and Don Macke. "Wealth in Missouri and Its Counties." Lincoln, NE: Center for Rural Entrepreneurship, April 2013.

Brennan, Morgan. "America's Friendliest Towns." Forbes.com, December 19, 2012.

Burd, Charlynn, Alison Fields, and Michael Ratcliffe. "Defining Rural and the U.S. Census Bureau: American Community Survey and Geography Brief." Census.gov, issued December 2016.

Carr, Patrick J., and Maria J. Kefalas. *Hollowing out the Middle: The Rural Brain Drain and What It Means for America.* Boston: Beacon, 2009.

"The Divide between Rural and Urban in America in Six Charts." *U.S. News and World Report*, March 20, 2017.

Drake, Ron. *Flip This Town: Preservation Made Practical on Main Street USA.* Siloam Springs, AK: Ron Drake Consulting, 2013.

"El Dorado Promise Celebrates Success of 10th Anniversary." http://www.ElDoradoPromise.com/news, January 20, 2017.

"Firehouse Coffee Shop Has St. James Buzzing." Community Foundation of the Ozarks, http://www.cfozarks.org/firehouse-coffee-shop-has-st-james-buzzing/, August 30, 2011.

Gladwell, Malcolm. *Outliers: The Story of Success*. Boston: Little Brown, 2008.

Henderson, Anne T., and Karen L. Map. *A New Wave of Evidence: The Impact of Schools, Family, and Community Connections on Student Achievement*. Austin, TX: National Center for Family and Community Connections with Schools, 2002.

Longworth, Richard. *Caught in the Middle: America's Heartland in the Age of Globalism*. New York: Bloomsbury, 2008.

"Penney Store Closes in Founder's Hometown." *New York Times*, originally published June 9, 1981.

Shevlin, Ron. "Community Banks: Dethroned by Decaffeinated Deposits?" Insight Vault: Cornerstone Advisors, http://www.crnrstone.com, February 12, 2018.

Shickley Community Foundation Annual Newsletter, December 2016.

"Volunteers Are an Important Part of a System of Student and Learning Supports." Center for Mental Health in Schools and Student Learning Supports at UCLA, http://www.smhp.psych.ucla.edu.

Zhang, Yu. "Covering Local Community Banks: Trends and Stats." http://www.BusinessJournalism.org, April 25, 2017.

ABOUT THE AUTHOR

Andrew McCrea

ANDREW MCCREA is the host of the *American Countryside* radio broadcasts. His features have won numerous awards for broadcast excellence and are seen and heard nationally. His journalism work began with an unpaid internship over two decades ago. Today, five thousand episodes later, *American Countryside* is in print, heard on the radio, and seen on television. In addition, McCrea is a nationally recognized speaker, entertaining and motivating audiences from coast to coast. He and his family reside on the family farm and ranch in northwest Missouri, where he remains active in the daily operations.